Men, Women and Violence

A Collection of Papers from CODESRIA Gender Institute 1997

Men, Women and Violence

*A Collection of Papers from
CODESRIA Gender Institute 1997*

Edited by Felicia Oyekanmi
Director Gender Institute 1997

Council for the Development of Social Science Research in Africa

Men, Women and Violence

© Council for the Development of Social Science Research in Africa 2000
Avenue Cheikh Anta Diop, Angle Canal IV,
P.O. Box 3304, Dakar, Senegal

ISBN : 2-86978-077-X
ISBN-13: 978-2-86978-077-4

Typesetting: Hadijatou Sy
Printed by Lightning Source

Published and distributed by CODESRIA and
The African Books Collective

CODESRIA would like to acknowledge the support of the Swedish Agency for International Development Cooperation Agency (SIDA/SAREC), the International Development Research Centre (IDRC), the Ford Foundation, the MacArthur Foundation, the Carnegie Corporation, the Norwegian Ministry of Foreign Affairs, the Danish Agency for International Development (DANIDA) the French Ministry of Cooperation, the United Nations Development Programme (UNDP), the Netherlands Ministry of Foreign Affairs, the Rockefeller Foundation, and the Government of Senegal in its research, training and publications programmes.

Contents

Preface vii

Towards Research into Wife Battering in Ghana:
  Some Methodological Issues 1
Henrietta Abane

Domestic Violence in Kenya: A Survey of
  Newspaper Reports 25
Mumbi Machera

Gender Differentials in Students' Perception
  and Participation in Violence: A Case Study of the
  University of Lagos 51
Funmi Bammeke

Sociocultural Implications of Wife Beating
  Among the Yoruba in Ibadan City, Nigeria 77
Morayo Atinmo

Women and the Dialectic of War: A Comparative
  Study of the Portrayal of Women in the Nigerian
  Civil War Fiction 123
Augustine Uzoma Nwagbara

Aspects of Gender Violence in Urban Market
  Gardening in Metropolitan Lagos, Nigeria 151
Emmanuel E. Adjekophori

Bibliography 177

Preface

Gender-based violence — mainly by men on women, but also by women on men and between members of the same sex — is alarmingly widespread across a variety of cultures. It has been and remains prevalent in so-called traditional societies, in Africa and elsewhere, and is also apparently on the increase in developed societies.

Violence against women in particular is a global problem, in the home, in the neighbourhood and at work, with rape, assault, wife battering and beating, and sexual harassment among the most obvious manifestations. These are recognised as gross violations of human rights by the United Nations and other world bodies. An international bill of rights for women, the Convention on the Elimination of all Focus of Discrimination Against Women (CEDAW), was adopted by the United Nations as long ago as 1979, and over 160 countries are party to it. In addition, women are protected by the Convention Against Torture and other Cruel, Inhuman or Degrading Treatment or Punishment (CAT) 1984 and the Declaration on the Protection of All Persons from Being Subjected to Torture and other Cruel, Inhuman or Degrading Treatment or Punishment (1975). Yet the problem at grassroots is getting worse throughout the world.

Men, Women and Violence is a selection of papers resulting from the 1997 CODESRIA Gender Institute, which gathered researchers and resource persons from Benin, Cameroon, Ghana, Kenya, Nigeria, Senegal, Sudan, Uganda and the United States. The collection is a contribution to the continuing debate on gender-based violence, with case studies from West and East Africa. The contributors highlight how universal attitudes of male dominance and patriarchy can literally engender a culture of violence in which women and children are the victims. There are often no laws or customs to prevent wife beating, to take one example, and indeed to engage in it is regarded as conduct, conformable and a routine expression of male dominance. Being often domestic in nature and in the private domain, acts of violence and aggression are seldom reported and leave the victims with no redress, except to `suffer in silence' or retaliate with grave consequences.

This arena of social enquiry is in its initial stages in Africa, with few statistics and resources or even appropriate legislation in place. One respondent in Ibadan cited in these pages challenged his interviewer: 'If I decide to beat my wife to death, how does that concern you?' Patriarchal attitudes and the gender bias that underpin violent acts will not be changed in a day or without resistance. Yet a start is being made, and publication of case study research like the present volume is vital if the issue of gender violence is to be taken out of the realm of privacy and silence and into public policy.

1. Towards Research into Wife Battering in Ghana: Some Methodological Issues

Henrietta Abane*

The recognition by the international community in the past decade that the benefits of development are not equally distributed within society and that women are not incorporated into the process, encouraged the institution of a new development perspective — sustainable human development (SHD). Wife battering represents a hidden obstacle to economic and social development. It saps women's energy, undermines their confidence and compromises their health, thus depriving society of women's full participation. The position of women within the Ghanaian family to a large extent is conditioned by traditional values and cultural beliefs of society which find expression in religion and legal systems and which are reinforced by formal education and the mass media. Any strategy to combat wife battering must attack the root causes of the problem, challenging social attitudes and beliefs that underlie male violence and renegotiating its meaning from the cultural contexts of the society. Any tools

---
* Department of Sociology, University of Cape Coast, Ghana.

used to gather information should give flexibility to respondents, who may want to render vivid accounts. Open-ended questions may elicit the most reliable responses to interviews, and focus group discussion will help the researcher gain insight into the world of batterers and their victims. A quantity of ethnographic data will be generated that may not be too easy to process. A qualitative method of analysis using the voices of respondents may be effective.

Violence against wives is an outcome of the belief, fostered in all cultures, that men are superior and that the women with whom they live are their possessions to be treated as they consider appropriate (Connors 1992:3).

INTRODUCTION

The period 1976-85, proclaimed the United Nations (UN) Decade for Women, had a plan of action with the goals of equality, development and peace. This marked a watershed in human resource development as it brought women, the other half of the world's population, into development. A more people-centred development paradigm – sustainable human development (SHD) – was adopted by countries world-wide and aimed at exploring new ways of improving the lives and conditions of the world's poor. SHD involved, among others, an improvement in the status of and the opening up of economic opportunities for women (UNDP 1995). It was realized that only when disparities in social, economic and political equality together with sex imbalances are addressed can an achievement in sustainable human development be made. In other words, a gendered approach to development was necessary if SHD was to be achieved. This gender approach was expected to address women's concerns within a socially constructed relationship between men and women and to consist of a set of tool.

Following this decade, various governments intensified efforts to shift women from the periphery to the centre of national development processes across Africa. This was generally hampered by women's unequal and subordinate positions, mainly from two factors. First is the co-existence of women's multiple roles as reproducer, producer and traditional manager of resources; Second is the gender discriminatory cultural beliefs that infiltrate institutions at various levels of society (UNDP 1995). These have a direct impact on women's lives in terms of their share in power and decision making at the household, community and national levels and access to and participation in education, health care, employment, land and property ownership, credit and shelter. Thus, one finds a case of male bias permeating all parts of the African socioeconomic structure.

In recent times women's movements, feminists and researchers have identified male violence against women as a big obstacle to women's participation in developmental processes in various countries. This has also been seen as an obstacle to peace, not to mention its implication for equality.

Male violence against women takes various forms. It could be symbolic, in discrimination owing to custom, tradition or law. It could be institutional violence, meted out from the state apparatus such as when the political rights of women are denied, women are raped in official custody, or the laws and military are used to brutalize women, as happened in Ghana in the aftermath of the 1979 and 1981 revolutions. Male-perpetuated violence against women could also be at a personal level, and sexual abuse occurs. Whatever the form male violence against women takes, it has been noted to make deep physical and psychological scars on women.

Perpetrators of violence feel justified and even seek social legitimation for their conduct, while victims tend to assume responsibility for their plight and resort to self-blame, shame and guilt. Battered women's psychological stress is seen to induce dependency, debility and dread, thereby breaking their personality, a process labelled variously as 'learned helplessness' (Walker 1979) and 'battered woman syndrome' (Steinmetze 1979). It is counter-argued that battered women do not become stereotypes of passivity, weakness, dysfunction and loss of agency implied by the term 'helplessness'. Rather, concrete constraints prevent them from leaving, for example, the community fails to respond and provide resources (Copelon 1994). The assertion made is that, as violence escalates, self-blame recedes and battered women realistically fear that leaving will precipitate what has been identified as 'separation assault' (Mahoney 1991) — the acute, violent and potentially lethal legal battle that accompanies the process of separation. For Blackmun (1989), the interaction of violence, terror and social and economic constraints narrow the framework of a woman's agency. She asserts that the societally based limitations of patriarchy; the psychological decrements in self-esteem; the high intensity of violent interactions; and the fear-induced restrictions; on an individual's ability to think in complex terms all contribute to chronic victims of wife abuse.

LITERATURE REVIEW

Existing theories in the explanation of violence are classified into three. These are intra-individual, social-psychological and sociocultural theories.

Intra-individual Theories

Intra-individual theories explain violence in terms of the individual actor. Some of these theories see personality abnormality or defects and alcohol and drug use as causing violent psychopathological tendencies in humans (Gelles and Strauss 1979). Others see chromosomes and hormones in males to be medically linked to violence. For instance, it is suggested that the chromosomes in males are productive of low intelligence which correlates with low educational levels, limited occupational opportunities and increased frustration to cause anti-social behaviour and violence (Jarvick *et al.* 1973). Studies have also found a causal relationship between aggression and levels of androgens such as testosterone (Dabbs and Morris 1990) and serotonin (Mckenry *et al.* 1995). Still other theories have linked organic brain syndrome to violent outbursts (Monroe 1970).

Certain gaps have been identified in the use of these theories. For instance, Scut (1991) identifies that alcohol may be associated with violence but does not cause it. In many families, drunkenness may occur without any violence being precipitated, while violence may occur without any alcohol being consumed. For Leonard and Blane (1992), the relationship between alcohol use and violence is moderated by both the man's level of hostility and level of marital satisfaction.

Social-psychological Theories

Social-psychological theories examine the interaction of the individual with the social environment, that is, with other individuals, groups and organizations.

The frustration—aggression theory views the expression of aggression either as a response to the emotion that an individual feels when some goal is blocked or as a response to frustration being the product of learning (Steinmetze 1988; Abraham 1995). Violence is seen to be highly related to social stress such as poverty and job loss. As a marriage declines in satisfaction, a growing sense of anger and frustration emerges that increases the potential for violence.

Social learning theory views violence as a learned phenomenon. Together with the role modelling theory, it assumes that children learn violent behaviour when they see their parents or other significant others resolving problems by means of violence (Abraham 1995). The children then model this role of violent interpersonal behaviour when they themselves become parents. Social learning theory is built around the use of reinforcement and extinction as well as association stimuli. When children see violence on the television, for instance, they become desensitized and no longer respond to environmental cues that inhibit their own tendencies towards violence. Thus people learn and internalize social and moral justifications for abusive behaviour.

Exchange theory asserts that marital interaction is governed by an attempt to maximize rewards and to minimize cost. Reward, for the perpetrators of wife abuse, may include the release of anger and frustration as well as the accumulation of power and control, while for the victim it may be economic benefit. The cost of violence includes the victim hitting back, arrest and/or imprisonment, over status among friends and relatives, and divorce or separation (Gelles and Cornell 1990). A related theory is resource theory, which explains that violence is used as a resource to gain one's wishes in a manner similar to the use of money, status and individual personal attributes (Steinmetze 1988). The extent of material resources controlled by husbands and wives determines their relative influence over major decisions and their control of marital power. According to Goode (1971), violence is the ultimate resource in that it is used when other resources are perceived to be insufficient or to have failed to obtain the desired response. Thus men who lack these other resources feel powerless and resort to force and violence, while women with a significant resources may be less willing to put up with abuse.

The conflict theory of violence assumes that conflict is an inevitable part of all associations which are characterized by super-ordinate and subordinate relations as well as competing goals. The family is viewed as an arena of confrontation and conflicting interests, and so violence is a likely outcome. For instance, social inequality is seen at play in the redistribution of family resources; where domestic labour is pooled within the family, men are seen to claim a greater share of domestic resources irrespective of who brings them in (Glenn 1987).

Sociocultural Theories

Sociocultural theories focus on macro-level analysis. Hence such theories place marital violence within a wider explanatory framework that considers the impact of social institutions and social structures on social behaviour.

Structural theory identifies the source of violence as stress, frustration and deprivation resulting from economic crises. People with fewer resources relative to other members of the society are known to experience higher levels of frustration and the stress. They also have fewer material, emotional, psychological and social resources to cope adequately. Frustration from material deprivation may result in physical wife abuse because the husband is limited in his ability to provide for his family and to meet normative expectations with poverty or unemployment, and the stress and frustration may result in his use of violence. Hence one would expect a greater prevalence of family violence among the poor, in large families and in crowded suburbs (Glenn 1987; Steinmetze 1988; Abraham 1995).

Marxist theory explains the source of violence from an economic and political perspective. Women are an oppressed economic class deprived of economic control, political power and status. They are victimised by the patriarchal capitalist system which fosters control of the oppressed class by their oppressors. Violence, then, is employed as the male's mechanism of controlling females (Mies 1986).

Feminist theory highlights the oppressive character of structural inequality based on gender. For feminists, gender itself is a social construction of male and female identified with unequal social value. The institution of patriarchy, a system of male dominance, conditions women psychologically into accepting a secondary status by embracing a process of sex-role stereotyping. While women are expected to be expressive in outlook, men are conditioned to demonstrate instrumental traits. Social pressure is seen to keep women conforming to the expressive role, a role of rationality and power (Eisenstein 1984; Sheffield 1987; Glenn 1987). Feminist theory criticizes male-female relationships as gendered constructions. Marital violence is seen as the most overt and effective means of husbands social control of wives, in that it is used when other and more subtle methods of control do not elicit submission (Hoffman et al. 1994:132). The problematic nature of marriage for women has been linked to its centrality in patriarchy, the devaluation of women's work and the hierarchy of gender (Glenn 1987; Feree 1990).

QUALITY OF LIFE

Gender-based violence is seen as a profound health problem for women across the globe. A *World Development Report* in 1993 also identified rape and domestic violence as significant causes of disability and death among women of reproductive age in both the industrial and developing world. The World Bank estimates that these account for 5 per cent of the healthy years of life lost to women in demographically developing countries (Heise *et al.* 1994).

The mental health consequences of wife beating identified include fear, anxiety, fatigue, post-traumatic stress disorder, and sleeping and eating disorders. Together with physical injuries, these totally destroy women, dehumanize them and set up a wilful, self-destructive mechanism, the negative impact on the quality of life being both severe and long term (Heise et al. 1994). Lauer (1989) also identifies that wife beating negatively affects the family fabric as family members fail to promote economic, social and emotional support to and for one another. In this sense, the family as society's basic social unit fails to focus on the well-being of its members. Gender-based violence has also been identified to have important implications for socioeconomic development. It is widely accepted that problems such as high fertility and hunger cannote be solved without women's full participation. Yet when they are burdened with the physical and psychological scars of abuse (Heise *et al.* 1994).

Violence against women is an overwhelming moral, economic and public health burden that societies can no longer bear and which the world should respond to.

HUMAN RIGHTS

The greatest restriction of liberty, dignity and movement and at the same time a direct violation of woman, is the threat and realization of violence (Bunch 1991:7). The narrow definition of human rights as a matter of state violation of civil and political liberties make governments trivialize women's rights concerns. Women's rights are considered secondary to the concerns of life and death, a myth which fails to admit that sexism kills. Violence against women is not personal or cultural. It is profoundly political for as long as it results from the structural relations of power, domination and privilege between men and women in society. Violence is central to maintaining those political relations at home, at work and in all public spheres. If violence and domination are understood as a politically constructed reality, then it is possible to imagine deconstructing the system to build a better and just interaction between the sexes (Bunch 1991). Specifically, wife battering is seen as a form of torture (Copelon 1994) that is an independent violation of human rights. In international human rights conventions, states are charged to address the cultural acceptance of gender-based discrimination as well as economic, political, social and cultural dis-entitlement that renders women vulnerable to violence and encumbers their capacity to escape it.

LITERATURE ON GHANA

No comprehensive research of the extent and nature of wife beating has been carried out in Ghana. Oppong (1974) sought to examine marital continuity and change among educated urban migrants of matrilineal descent. Two major aspects of the nuclear family relationship were compared. First was the division of labour, resources and power between spouses, and second the extent to which the conjugal family was a functionally discrete unit in a number of respects. Oppong's study failed to consider the use of physical and other forms of aggression employed by spouses during conflict. It also focused on kin relations as the major variable determining conflict.

Ofei-Aboagye's (1994) preliminary study of domestic violence in Ghana examined the role of tradition in perpetuating domestic violence as well as efforts made by existing organizations to expose and curb violence. A preliminary interview conducted on clients of the International Federation of Women Lawyers (FIDA − Ghana) revealed that some abused wives could no longer suffer violence silently. Most of them had gone to FIDA as all their attempts for redress had failed. Note was also taken of some aspects of Ghanaian culture and tradition that contributed to domestic violence not being acknowledged as a problem in the country. In this direction, Ofei-Aboagye researched oral traditions, folklore and proverbs of the Akan that served to entrench inequality between men and women.

Ampofo (1992) considered both state institutional and interpersonal violence against Ghanaian women. Forms of violence considered included domestic violence, widowhood rites, female genital mutilation, rape and military floggings during the Armed Forced Ruling Council (AFRC) revolution of 1979.

WIFE BATTERING: WORLD SCENARIO

Wife beating is very much under-reported and under-documented, hence its prevalence is also underestimated around the world. The few statistics available, however, reveal the gruesome nature of the act. In the USA alone, over 2 million women get battered each year (Benokraitis 1996). Violence is said to occur at least once in two-thirds of all marriages, while one out of every eight couples admitted that there had been an act of violence between them which caused serious injury, and that between 40 and 60 per cent of all police night calls were domestic disputes (Carrillo 1991).

Some 9500 and five million wife assault cases are reported annually in Sweden (Hyden 1994) and Germany (Ampofo 1992) respectively. In France, 95 per cent of victims of violence are women, while 25% of women cite battery as reason for divorce in Denmark (Carrillo 1991). The first report of the British Crime Survey found that 10 per cent of all assault victims were women who had been assaulted by their present or previous husband or lover. Analysis of assault on women in two Scottish villages in 1974 also revealed that wife assault was the second most common form of violent crime, accounting for 25 per cent of all crimes recorded by the police (UN 1989). In developing countries the pattern seems to be the same even though statistics on the extent of the problem are incomplete. Carrillo (1994) reports that in Chile, 80 per cent of women were found to be victims in a Santiago study; two-thirds of rural women in Korea were periodically beaten by their husbands. Furthermore, 50 per cent of all married women were regularly beaten in Thailand while in Pakistan 99 per cent of housewives and 77 per cent of working women were beaten by their husbands. Other reports have also found a high incidence of wife battering in such countries as Bangladesh, Colombia, Kenya, Kuwait, Nicaragua and Nigeria.

Despite issue of violence against women being raised at various international meetings, it was not until 1980 that increasing public awareness of the need to eliminate all forms of violence against women and children, including domestic violence, was fully reflected in the Copenhagen meeting on the UN Decade for Women (UN 1989; UNDP 1995). Themed equality, development and peace, the meeting acknowledged that domestic violence was a complex problem that constituted an intolerable offence to the dignity of human beings. In 1985, the Third World Conference in Nairobi also reviewed violence against women in the family. It adopted forward-looking strategies to put women in development programs and to remove at the national level all discriminatory laws against women. Gender issues were given prominence at the 1993 World Conference in Human Rights at Vienna. At this conference, women's rights were included in the Declaration and Program of Action on Violence Against Women which were adopted by the UN General Assembly in December

1993. The Beijing World Conference on Women held in 1995 also considered resolutions past conferences and sought ways in which affirmative action could be used by governments to emancipate women. It recommended the following among others: the adoption and implementation of legislation to end violence against women; and active work to ratify and implement all international agreements related to violence against women, including the UN Convention on the Elimination of All Forms of Discrimination Against Women (UN-CEDAW) adopted in 1979.

THE GHANAIAN SCENARIO

Marriage is a critical feature of Ghanaian social and economic life. All men and women are expected to marry and all women to procreate. Marriage and family life are expected to be fulfilling and functional not only for the contracting spouses, but also for their families and society as a whole. Successful marriages give emotional support and have psychological advantages for the whole family. Domestic violence, unfortunately, is on the ascendancy in most families across cultures, negating the myth of the family as a warm and loving place in which members care and nurture one another (Cadwallader 1973; Eitzen and Zinn 1992). Marital conflict has emerged, with its associated tensions and stresses not only as a result of the pressures and burdens of marital expectations, but also as a result of some factors external to the family unit.

One important area in which marital and family life have been profoundly affected is that of social change.

Social change has occurred as a consequence of western culture, politics, religions, science, economic specialisation, technological expansion, education, transportation, schools and new methods of conquering nature which have led to large-scale migration and urbanisation (Gwonde-Kaunda 1990; Adler 1992; Byfield 1996; Ocholla-Ayayo 1997). It has weakened family bonds and encouraged individualism, marginalised and frustrated husbands; encouraged divorce, teenage pregnancies and indiscipline among children; pauperisation of families; and social upheaval, theft and violence. Modernisation has brought many families and individuals in Africa into situations entirely unknown in traditional lifestyles, uprooting them out of the context of corporate morality, customs and traditional solidarity (Ocholla-Ayayo 1997).

In Ghana, wife beating is a man's way of teaching the wife a lesson, and even women have shown less sympathy for victims of wife beating who, according to custom, should learn to be cautious and calm (Ofei-Aboagye 1994). Although there are cultural mechanisms for intervening in battery situations in marriage, men as heads of households are still expected to use some form of discipline if need be to bring sanity into their households. Women are therefore socialized to accept physical and emotional chastisement as a husband's marital prerogative. Ghanaian culture by and large perceives women as inferior beings who can be used and battered at will. This situation is largely portrayed by data obtained from FIDA of Ghana. This group categorized cases that it handled into child custody, maintenance, family reconciliation, marital and cases of paternity. The total number of cases handled by FIDA rose from 300 in 1990 to 1 047 in 1995. Marital cases rose steadily from 46 (representing 12.2 per cent of total cases) in 1991 through 141 (16.2 per cent) in 1994 to 192 (24.9 per cent) in 1995.

The growing number of cases reported indicates that perhaps this is just the tip of the iceberg and therefore gives rise for concern. The subordinate position of women within Ghanaian culture has largely been shaped by the people's traditional beliefs and values, which find expression in oral tradition, folktales and music (Ofei-Aboagye 1994). The social legitimation given to wife beating can even be seen within the legal framework of the country. The police and judiciary have been gender insensitive in their handling of male violence against women. Victims who seek redress through these avenues become ridiculed and frustrated as they are encouraged to make an out-of-court settlement (Ampofo 1992).

The Ghanaian Cultural Experience

Ghana is a multi-cultural society in which across cultures, traditional values and beliefs discriminate against women, making them unequal to their male counterparts, and giving women a very low status in society. Some examples will be drawn from the Akan culture with which this researcher is familiar.

Sayings
A musket is fired from a man's chest.
The clarion call for people goes out to men.
It is the man who markets the woman's livestock.

These sayings indicate either the bravery or importance of men. In the third saying a father, however irresponsible, has the right to receive bride-wealth on his daughter's wedding day.

Folktales

Most Akan folktales are told to teach a moral. It is common especially within the traditional set-up, to find both adults and children gathered around an evening fire listening to tales from an elder. It is usually within this same setting that folksongs related to the tales are taught. The most popular of such tales are the Ananse stories. Most folktales portray men as chauvinists with an unchallenged mandate to control their households (Ofei-Aboagye 1994). Women are depicted as weak and submissive, without any rights whatsoever within the family.

Highlife Music

Together with folksongs, highlife music is used to buttress the message given in sayings and folktales. It tends, to celebrate male infidelity and warn females to be chaste, making women unequal to men (Ofei-Aboagye 1994). While some depict women as sex objects, others stress their domestic roles. For instance, 'Soja Alafia' by A, B, Cretentsil, literally translated, calls on a woman named Ajoa to lift up her leg because the soldier's bitter medicine is sweet.

Gyedy Blay Ambolley's 'Akokoba' also translates to mean top making noise, chicken, your mother has nowhere to go but under this basket shows that whatever the case women are confined to one position or role, that of homemaker.

It may be found, then, that the corpus of myths, symbols, tales, sayings and proverbs is the medium through which constraint, obedience, shame, submission and fear are socialised in gender relations (Mama 3/96).

Studying Wife Battering: Methodological Issues

There is the need for research aimed at identifying the sociocultural and socioeconomic correlates of marital conflict. It should attempt to answer the following research questions:

(1) What are the forms of battering wives endure?
(2) What are the specific causes of wife beating?
(3) What part if any do traditional values and cultural beliefs play in encouraging wife beating?
(4) What are the effects of battering on wives?
(5) What are the social costs of wife beating?
(6) What measures can be taken by society to address the problem?

The research should be geared towards sensitizing the general public, government officials and policy makers, the police and judiciary as to the gravity of the problem. It should stimulate discussion of wife beating at all levels of the society and awaken women in particular to address the cultural beliefs that put them in disadvantageous positions within marriage. Furthermore, such research should make recommendations on how victims of wife beating may be helped to get over the trauma as well as changes in the penal code system to deter husbands from engaging in the act.

It is submitted that much as the various explanations of wife battering of violence against women generally are valid, there is the need to apply them in various combinations while not losing sight of the Ghanaian social context within which the violence occurs. A conceptual model of marital conflict therefore may be suggested within which the following factors may be explored : alcohol, employment status, educational status, stress, poverty, gender roles, role of in-laws and other kinsmen, conflict over children and or stepchildren, irritable behaviour such as undesirable friends, and the role of traditional values and cultural beliefs in promoting marital conflict. Ethnic or cultural differences between spouses may also be a source of conflict in many families. This is because an act which is culturally acceptable in one instance may be provocative in another. Decision making over most important issues in a relationship will to a large extent reveal the nature of marital power and hence conflict. All these variables should be examined within the broad context of structural inequality between men and women in the society.

Research into wife battering in Ghana may is the first instance be difficult to pursue given the very 'private' nature of the family and the fact that traditionally, it is improper for one to wash dirty linen in public. The accuracy of data to be gathered thus will depend on the quality of interaction between the interviewer and the interviewee, and in particular, the ability of the former to infuse a sense of trust, safety and intimacy into the interviewing relationship (Smith 1994:116).

Secondly, the very concept of wife battering may be difficult to define since in some Ghanaian cultures some forms of abuse such as a push, slap, arm twisting, aggressive holding and many more may not be viewed as acts of battery. Besides, though marital rape occurs with an incidence of battery or separately (UN 1989), there is no such thing as marital rape within the culture. The very giving of gifts in the form of bride-wealth to the parents of kinsmen of the woman during the marital negotiations gives the husband unrestricted access not only to the labour of his wife, but also sexual services. Thus if not properly structured, the others may conceal the actual dimensions of the problem. Violence then becomes something which can be defined only against the backdrop of culture, tradition and custom.

Thirdly, there is the problem of identification of sources of conflicts within the family. Since variables identified in the literature (mainly from the developed world) may be seen either to intensify or actually precipitate conflict and battery situations, there is the need to go beyond these to search for factors within the Ghanaian context. Some of these factors have already been discussed in the previous section of this article.

DATA COLLECTION

Both primary and secondary sources of data should be used in the proposed study. Secondary data may be obtained from FIDA (Ghana), the Department of Social Welfare and the Police Service. Hospital records, family tribunals and divorce courts may also yield some information, but these may be inadequate for a thorough investigation into the problem of marital conflict and wife battering. In the case of hospital records, a lot of information may be lost if injuries treated are not labelled as domestic assault injuries. Again, though reports may be lodged with the same officials, and may be lodged with the same officials and may be unwilling to attend family tribunals. Furthermore, since most marriages are contracted customarily, not many of these find their way into divorce courts in the event of divorce. The suggested groups, therefore, are known to have a rich database on material conflict and wife battering that would be useful in analyzing trends.

Primary data may be collected with two main tools, a general survey and focus group discussions. A general survey is important to measure the incidence and prevalence of wife battering with the help of a structured interview schedule. The following may be worth noting:

(1) A major methodological problem in victimization surveys is the under-reporting of abuse. The subject of wife beating may be too personal, or respondent may be embarrassed; she might forget minor battery incidences or they may be too minor to merit attention. Respondent may also be too traumatized to discuss follow-up questions. When surveys are under-reported, the results are put into jeopardy as the disclosure figure may not be representative

of the victims in the sample. Secondly, under-reporting also has negative implications for social policy because the probability for mobilizing funds is lowered (Smith 1994).

(2) Use open-ended questions. This elicits the most valid and reliable responses. Open-ended questions also build interviewer — respondent rapport and may reduce the power imbalance inherent in an interview situation. This technique encourages interaction and collaboration between the interviewer and respondent (Hanmer and Saunders 1984; Hoff 1990).

(3) In order to estimate the prevalence of wife battering, there is the need to query a respondent's possible involvement more than once in different ways, and at a different points in the survey. This is because some respondents are unable to indicate they are victimised at the first broach of the subject, but only toward the end of the interview, usually while answering another related question (Smith 1994).

Furthermore, there is the need to focus on whether the respondent has ever been battered in both his or her adult life or in marriage, and perhaps if batterings occurred in the past year. Such use of life-time estimates usually increases the size of the sample of reported victims. It also provides a surer footing for investigating the causes and consequences of victimization (Sesser 1990).

(4) Finally, there is the need to investigate the context and consequences of violence to adequately understand wife battery in the interview.

These interviews must be conducted by people specially trained to acquire interviewing skills as well as empathetic attitudes. They should be gender-sensitive at all times, establish rapport and be able to ask threatening questions without making the respondents hold back accounts.

In addition to the general survey, two focus group discussions (FGD) for males and females respectively may be organized. FGD sessions stimulate debate and the generation of multiple descriptions and explanation of reality (Bilson 1997). Here, the structural base for male domination and female subordination that breeds inequality within marriage and that ultimately leads to conflict and battery may be brain-stormed. Men will have the opportunity to tell their side of the story so as to put the whole issue of conflict and battery into perspective. The discussion can also help women overcome their structural isolation and realise that their individual sufferings have social causes and are in some ways shared by other women (Bilson 1991). These discussions may be taped and later transcribed.

It is possible to generate a quantity of ethnographic data using these two methods as outlined above. It is therefore suggested that a qualitative methods of analysis be employed. Wherever possible the voices of both men and women should be used while protecting their identities. This will go a long way to enriching the analysis and bring to the fore the gravity of the problem being investigated.

CONCLUSION

Violence against women generally is seen to cut across cultures, class and religion. It is the only thing that binds all women be they in the First, Second or Third Worlds. Violence prevents women from contributing their quota towards the development of their countries. The family, which is supposed to be the safe haven for most people, unfortunately has become a nightmare for most women. The actual nature and extent of spouse beating, especially wife beating, is uncertain in Ghana. This article has sought to present the problem of wife beating and emphasised the need for research which takes into consideration some conceptual and methodological issues. It is sincerely hoped that this challenge would be taken up.

2. Domestic Violence in Kenya: A Survey of Newspaper Reports

Mumbi Machera [*]

INTRODUCTION

'Domestic violence' is the term used to describe a variety of actions that occur in family relationships. According to the United Nations (1990), the term is used narrowly to cover incidents of physical attacks. It may take the form of physical and sexual violations, such as punching, checking, stabbing, scalding and burning with water and acid, or setting a blaze, the results of which can range from bruising to death. Domestic violence also includes psychological or mental violence, which can consist of repeated verbal abuse, harassment, confinement and deprivation of physical, financial and personal resources.

According to Davies (1994), the term domestic violence is sometimes used to describe violence against women in the family while in other instances it is used as a general label covering any violation where the victim and the perpetrator have some form of personal and family

---
[*] Department of Sociology, University of Nairobi, Kenya.

relationship or where they have had a relationship in the past. Used in this wider sense, domestic violence encompasses child abuse, be it physical, psychological or sexual, violence between siblings, abuse or neglect of the elderly, abuse of children by their parents, violence between marital partners, and violence between members of the same sex in the family.

Domestic violence was first established as a development issue at the United Nations Decade for Women's meeting in Nairobi in 1985. Since then, international organisations and locally based agencies, and individual activists across the world have campaigned vigorously against abuses such as rape, wife beating, sexual slavery and harassment among others.

Nevertheless, countries as far apart as the United States of America, Zimbabwe, Brazil, France and the Philippines have seen the issue of domestic violence raised on to the political agenda. In some of these countries, new laws have been implemented to extend and protect women's rights.

In spite of these efforts, domestic violence is still the most common and widespread form of violence throughout the world. Studies have shown that women and children constitute the majority of the victims. They often get hurt, thus making domestic violence tantamount to violence against women (Borkowski *et.al.* 1983; El Husseiny 1987; Dobash and Dobash 1979; Daly and Wilson 1988). It has also been established that domestic violence is gender-based because violence against women in the family is rooted in the structural relationships of power domination and privilege existing between men and women in different societies. Thus women, being generally subordinated by the patriarchal systems which prevail in most parts of the world, are rendered powerless and defenceless in the face of domestic violence.

Because of the hidden nature of the problem, research on domestic violence is fairly new and has been undertaken perhaps only in the last 25 years. Research into this area originated in Western Europe, North America, Australia and New Zealand.

An increasing number of studies are now being undertaken in the developing world. The following study is a contribution towards the study of domestic violence in Kenya.

Problem Statement and Justification

Domestic violence is an anti-development phenomenon that occurs in almost every society. Its effects range from physical injuries to death. It has been noted, for example, that abused women suffer from health and psychological problems. They have a significantly higher level of anxiety, depression and somatic complaints than women who have not suffered abuse (Jaffe *et al.* 1986). Such women are often paralysed by terror from the ever-present threat of an attack and are more likely to commit suicide than those women who have not been battered (Hilberman and Munson 1987; Stark *et al.* 1979). It has also been suggested that the adverse consequences of domestic violence are not confined to the victim alone but the abuser himself may suffer the consequences of his behaviour. Research indicates that the women who kill their husbands do so more often than not in response to an immediate attack or threat (Ranjana 1991; Bacon and Lansdowne 1982).

According to UNIFEM (1992), Kenya has the highest rate of wife battering in Africa. Going by newspaper reports, it is also apparent that there is an existing escalating trend in the reporting of cases of gender-based domestic violence in the last 20 years, and this is threatening the stability of the highly valued family life and women's contribution to development. For example, in 1983 the world awakened to the shocking news about Piah Njoki, a Kenyan woman, whose eyes were gouged out by her husband, assisted by two other male relatives apparently for giving birth to daughters only, (Mama 1989). Such cases have become quite common in Kenya.

Against this background, it is crucial that detailed scientific research be conducted to establish the reasons behind increasing family violence as well as to investigate possible strategies which can be adopted to stop the problem. It should also be noted that only severe cases of domestic violence are reported in the newspapers, and the less severe ones such as wife beating, which are more common, are rarely reported.

OBJECTIVES OF THE STUDY

(1) To extract all the cases of domestic violence reported in the three daily newspapers[1] between 1 January 1997 and 30 June 1997.

(2) To categorise and analyse the forms of domestic violence reported during the six month period.

(3) To examine the causes of domestic violence reported during the six month period.

(4) To assess the underlying implications of the trends and patterns of domestic violence in Kenya and compare the existing situation with results obtained from other countries around the world.

Conceptualisation and Operationalisation of Terms

For the purposes of this study, the term domestic violence was taken to refer to the following forms of violence in a family relationship:

- Violence against women by men;
- Violence against children by family members;
- Violence against men by women;
- Violence between women;
- Violence between men;
- Children's violence against parents.

Thus in this study, six categories representing different family relationships in which violence occurs were conceptualised as mentioned above.

Consequently, the term violence was conceptualised as any reported act of attack by one person on another carried out with the intention of causing physical pain and injury to another person, mental anguish and even death. Subsequently the various forms of violence were operationalised as follows:

a) Violence against women by men—refers to abuse[2] of women by their male family members such as husbands, fathers, brothers or any other male relative.

b) Violence against children by family members—refers to abuse of children by their parents, brothers, sisters or any other relative.

c) Violence against men by women—refers to abuse of men by their wives, mothers, mothers's sisters, or any other female relatives.

d) Violence between women—refers to abuse of women by other women family members such as violence against housemaids by their employers, violence against wives by their mothers-in-law and sisters, among others.

e) Violence between men—refers to abuse or men by other men, e.g. fighting between brothers or brother-in-law.

f) Children's violence against parents—refers to abuse of parents by their own children.

Research Methodology

i) Data collection procedure — The data for this study was collected from the three main daily newspapers published in Kenya between 1 January and 30 June 1997. These newspapers were available from the Jomo Kenyatta Memorial Library at the University of Nairobi. Thus library research or what is popularly referred to as secondary data collection was used.

ii) Data analysis procedure — The data was largely analysed qualitatively as is often done in content analysis. However, a summary of frequencies and percentages is also provided.

Data Presentation and Interpretation

General Results

In total seventy-one cases of domestic violence were reported in the newspapers between the months of January and June 1997. Of these, 37 were cases of violence against children and 28 were cases of violence against women by men in the family. An average of twelve cases were reported per month, and over half of these concerned women and children as victims of domestic violence. All the reported cases were severe in nature, thus confirming that only the most serious cases of domestic violence are reported by the media. Table 1 below contains the total number of cases reported during that period by the month when reports were published.

Table 1: Number of Cases Reported During the Period

Month	Number of Cases Reported
January	21
February	12
March	5
April	7
May	13
June	13
Total	71

Source: Research Findings 1997.

The highest number of cases were reported in the month of January. Interestingly, studies done elsewhere have established a link between a rise in domestic violence and lack of financial resources like money. In Kenya, January is a time of the year when families are financially unstable after spending on the Christmas festivities and New Year school fees payment. Though this may not be the case, it is more likely to be one of the causes of high rates of domestic violence at the beginning of the year. For example, a recent report by the Convention for the Elimination of Discrimination Against Women (CEDAW) noted that women are `invisible victims' of the world economic crisis. Davies (1994) noted that one of the major ways in which women suffer from increased violence in times of economic crisis is through increased violence from their husbands. Research from Chile points to the subsistence existence and economic dependence of many families involved in domestic abuse (ISIS 1986). Research done in Nigeria indicates the economic deprivation and oppression of individuals leading to social injustice (Shamin 1987). Such violence is vented against the most powerless, who are inevitably women.

As is shown on Table 2, of the 21 cases of domestic violence reported in January, 7 or 33 per cent involved violence against children, whereas 6 or 29 per cent involved violence against women by men. Table 2 below contains a breakdown of the reported cases of violence (in different categories) by the month when they were reported.

Specific Research Findings

Violence Against Women

During the six-month period among the most frequently reported cases of violence against women by men in the family included wife battering and murder. Since only the severe forms of domestic violence attract the attention of the media, the less severe forms of violence against women such as wife beating are rarely reported. In this study, it was found that women are generally subjected to inhuman and life-threatening forms of abuse by men in the family. For example, the following incidents were reported in the country's dailies:

Ms Pamela Odira had her buttocks slashed with a panga[3] by her new husband. After interviewing this woman the press found that she was newly wedded and she did not know why the husband decided to treat her in such a cruel manner (DN, 8 January 1997).

Table 2: Reported Cases of Violence by Different Category

	VAWM	VAC	VAMW	VBW	VBM	CVAP
January	6	7	3	0	5	0
February	3	8	1	0	0	0
March	2	0	1	0	1	1
April	2	3	0	0	1	1
May	3	5	3	1	1	0
June	4	3	2	1	3	0
Total	20(28.2)	26(36.6)	10(14.2)	2(2.8)	11(15.5)	2(2.8)

Source: Research Findings 1997

NB: The abbreviations on the table are as follows:
VAWM: Violence Against Women by Men;
VAC: Violence Against Children Women's Violence Against Men;
VBM: Violence Between Men
CVAP: Children's Violence Against Parents.

In another incident,

> a primary school teacher in Kendu Bay [on the sources of Lake Victoria, Nyanka Province][4] allegedly beat his wife to death after she asked for money to buy their child milk. The woman was hit with metal bar on the head and was pronounced dead on arrival at the hospital (TS, 16 Feb.1997).

In another incident,

> a lab 60 years of age, killed his wife over land matters. The man slashed his wife after she objected the sale of family land (DN, 4 March 1997).

In another bizarre incident it was reported that

> a 50-year-old man stabbed his wife to death and drained her blood in a bucket after she allegedly refused to give him 2500 shillings (about $US 37) which he had given her to keep (KT, 13 June 1997).

These reports indicate the presence of a growing social malaise which should be of major concern. Existing gender inequalities in society accompanied by beliefs enforced by patriarchal kin systems give the male members of the society supremacy over women. Men are generally socialised to believe that women are property to be owned by men. Therefore a husband feels that he has access and control over the wife. It is no wonder that most men find the issue of punishing women normal and some go to the extent of killing them. Other reasons for violence against women may be economic, social and psychological. Though the newspaper reporting does not elaborate on causes of domestic violence, going by the terse information provided, it is clear that in most cases domestic quarrels over family economic resources such as land and money lead to serious consequences, and more often it is the women who get hurt. Other incidents indicate that expectations over social values such as sexual morality, marital faithfulness and paternity of offspring are increasingly becoming major sources of domestic violence which affects women adversely. For example, in one of the incidents, it was reported that:

> a man on Monday dismembered a month-old baby before chopping off the wife's arms with an axe following a bitter quarrel over the paternity of the child (KT, 29 May 1997)

However, the severity with which violence is executed upon women suggests that some of the perpetrators could be mentally ill. Though there is no proof to support this hypothesis (perpetrators are normally not taken for medical check-up) the possibility cannot be ruled out in some cases.

Violence Against Children

The study found that majority of the cases of domestic violence over the six-month period involved children as victims. However, in many societies, a certain amount of violence against children (referred to as discipline) is socially condoned. The situation in Kenya as reported in the newspapers reveals the extremely severe forms of violence which children are being subjected to. Such violence against children in the family goes beyond the realms of discipline. For example, in one of the reports:

> a primary school teacher assaulted her nine-year old son using a rungu[5], breaking both his legs besides inflicting several bruises and cuts on the youngsters back and head. The boy was apparently being punished for visiting his father who has since separated from his mother (KT, 8 May 1997).

More often, children become victims of domestic violence when they are caught in a crossfire or fights involving their parents. After serious domestic quarrels and fights, some parents vent their anger by punishing their innocent and defenceless children severely. For example, in one of the reports:

> a man hacked his child to death and seriously injured his wife after a domestic quarrel in Gatitu village, Maragua—District (DN, 28 February 1997).

In a related incident, one of the newspapers reported that:

> a couple abandoned their two children at the law courts in Mombassa. The man and his wife failed to reach an agreement on the children's upkeep after the case was adjourned (TES, 8 February 1997).

Such cases reflect on economic hardships which many breaking and stable families go through in developing countries. Children are most affected when marriages fail because in most cases they are left with the mother, who has no resources to cater for the growing children. Such children are likely to be subjected to child labour in and outside the family to assist their mother earn a living for them. For those women who remarry, they more often than not are not forced to leave their children with the parents or relatives. Such children do not grow up normally owing to lack off parental love and support. Consequently, if they follow the mother to her new marital home, they are likely to be subjected to discrimination and other forms of abuse because of their paternity.

The issue of paternity and its relation to violence against children in the family has raised major concern in Kenya. Often husbands, with or without proof take it upon themselves to punish the suspected spouse through beating or even killing them. Such `unwanted children' always get caught in such conflict. For example,

> police arrested a man who strangled his child. The man is believed to have strangled his two-month old son during a domestic quarrel in which he claimed the child was illegitimate (TES, 11 February 1997). Such cases are quite common.

Other common cases of domestic violence against children in Kenya include arranged early marriages, child abandonment after birth, ritual murders, incest and excessive beating. The *Daily Nation* reported that:

> a nine-year old girl was married off to a boy of the same age by the father who had borrowed six cows from the boy's father and had given the girl as security for the animals. Apparently the girl's father had sold the animals and thus the girl could not go back.

Early child marriage is a gender-based practice which is quite common among some ethnic groups in Kenya. In these tribes, girls are seen as less important than boys. Actually from birth, a girl is prepared for marriage. As a result, among the Samburu and Maasai of Kenya it is common practice to withdraw girls as young as nine years old from school for marriage. These groups view girls as assets, and a man counts his daughters in terms of the cows or cash he would receive as bridewealth in future. On the contrary, boys even though they are likely to have early marriages arranged for them, are allowed to continue with education to the highest level possible. Though the government in some cases moves to rescue the girls for the sake of their progress in education, such practices continue because of the strong cultural and social values associated with it.

In another report:

> a girl was ritually murdered in a chilling human sacrifice allegedly masterminded by a woman relative who wanted the spirits to guarantee her own children success in education. This incident took place in Mombasa (TES, 21 January 1997).

Killing of children for ritualistic and supernatural reasons is an age-old custom among some ethnic groups in Kenya. For example, among the Luo of Nyanza province, a now-extinct custom necessitated killing of twins soon after birth. The society believed that twins were a bad omen to such families. Such unfortunate babies were abandoned in the bush to be devoured by wild animals. More recently, some emerging religious sects have been associated with ritualistic murders of children. Such children are sacrificed by their parents or close relatives who believe in supernatural manifestations in the form of riches or financial benefits after the sacrifices have been offered.

Child abandonment is another common form of violence against children. About twenty years ago, the issue of child abandonment was still common and was mainly as a result of pregnancies conceived out of wedlock. Societal norms among most ethnic groups restricted girls from engaging in premarital sex, to preserve their virginity and reproductive functions till after marriage. Those girls who got pregnant were thus caught in a trap and often dumped the infants in bushes, latrines, rubbish pits etc. Today, such reasons persist but the HIV/AIDS pandemic has led to escalating trends of child abandonment. Newspapers often carry reports on mothers who escape from hospital leaving their HIV-positive babies behind. In a related incident, the report said that:

> a middle-aged woman in Kisewe village, Kitui District was arrested by police after she gave birth and threw the baby on the banks of a seasonal river (KT, January 1997).

Excessive beating of children is another form of domestic violence cited in the newspapers. Whereas moderate child beating is partly viewed as an acceptable disciplinary measure in most societies, sometimes parents have reportedly subjected their children to physical punishment which can be termed criminal in nature. For example, in one of the reports,

> a mother tortured her 14-year-old daughter to death and secretly buried her. Allegedly, the mother tied the girl's hands and legs with ropes before breaking her legs. She then hit her on the head with a metal bar. The girl had reportedly run away from home and returned the following day.

The issues discussed in this section indicate a need to focus attention on children as victims of domestic violence. In the past, violence against women has been the major focus for feminist activist groups. Yet it seems that women cannot enjoy freedom from domestic violence if their defenceless children are subjected to violence in the family. Ironically, women have been reported as being perpetrators of severe forms of violence against children.

Violence Between Women

This is a more hidden form of domestic violence. This study revealed a 28 per cent representation of this type of violence. Compared to violence against women by men, the occurrence is quite low. However, many women have reported being harassed physically and psychologically by their female family members. Many women complain of torture by their mothers-in-law. In most African countries, and in Kenya in particular, many ethnic groups still value the extended family system. As a result, when a woman gets married, she is responsible not only to her husband and children but also to the members of his family. The mother-in-law in particular, is very powerful and can have much control over her son's marriage. Since every human being enjoys some degree of independence and privacy, often the daughter-in-law finds herself at loggerheads with the senior woman; sometimes husbands have battered their wives over allegations by mothers and sisters in law. In some communities, senior women have the mandate to physically harass the younger wives (1992; Gallin 1992). Such violence more often than not creates a lifetime of rivalry and marital instability in families.

Another emerging form of violence between women involves women employers and their housemaids. Quite often, newspapers carry reports of cases whereby housemaids have been tortured by their employers (women). This happens both in the rural and urban areas. For example, one of the more common cases runs as follows:

> a house-girl aged 17 years old working for a family in Umoja Two Estate in Nairobi was scalded with boiling water by her employer. The woman suspected the house-girl of having an affair with the husband (KT, May 1997).

Violence between women is as anti-development as violence against women by men. Violence between women outside the home is also rampant. In the rural areas, communal development work is often hampered by what can be referred to as 'village gossip'. When women maliciously back bite each other, such feuds end up destroying vital relationships useful for community development. Though such issues are often disregarded and labelled as 'trivial', their impact can be detrimental. In urban areas women executives have been blamed for victimising their junior female staff members by undercutting their professional growth. This is quite ironic in the current events of global sisterhood and the improvement of women's status as an issue of not only global but national concern. This sort of violence is more often psychological than physically inclined.

Violence Between Men

Going by newspaper reports, violence between men in the family in Kenya is more common than violence between women. Of the cases gathered and analysed in this study, 15 per cent involved violence between men. A review of the cases reported showed that men are more inclined to physical violence. Such violence results after quarrels and disagreements over property and resources such as land inheritance. In most cases death is the end result. For example, in one of the reports,

> a family land feud involving a prominent Nairobi lawyer, his brothers and sisters almost turned tragic over the weekend when the lawyer and the brother attempted to run over each other using a tractor and a pick-up truck in Uasin Gishu [Rift-Valley Province District] (TES, 1 April 1997).

In another incident, which is characteristic of many other cases that often go unreported:

a 38-year-old man was sentenced to six month's imprisonment by the high court for killing his wife's lover (DN, June 1997).

The magnitude and diversity of escalating family violence can partly be attributed to the changing social, economic and cultural fabric of society. For example, whereas land feuds have become so common, in the traditional societies such matters were conveniently handled by the clan (Kenyatta, 1939). Today the clan system is no longer effective in most societies and has been substituted by the official judicial system. As a result family members can attempt to kill each other in order to overtake the court ruling in such matters.

Violence Against Men by Women

The issue of women's use of aggression against men is very controversial; both theoretical and practical examination of factors influencing gender relations in the society have attempted to focus on women as individual actors in the society. For example, ethnographic records suggest that in many societies, women are not simply passive victims of male violence, but have found a great many ways to even the score (Richters 1994). Sufferance co-exists with resentment, discontent, and instances of subordination. Women may become the accomplies of males inflicting violence against other women, especially at a later stage in life. Davies (1994) suggests the dynamics are usually very different when women kill their husbands or male partners. It is usually a response to years of male violence and not a culmination of years of female violence.

This study found that violence against men by women is common in Kenya but not as high as men's violence against women. Of the reported cases, 14.2 per cent involved women as perpetrators of violence in the family. In one of the reports, for example,

> a 49-year-old woman working with the Criminal Investigation Department fired three rounds of ammunition at her husband, killing him instantly after she caught him having an affair with another woman (TES, 15 June 1997).

In another incident,

> a civil servant's wife set their government house on fire at night while her husband, children and the housemaid were sleeping after a domestic quarrel (TES, January 1997).

Though women's aggression against men was a rare phenomenon in the traditional society in Africa, this trend is changing, not only in Kenya but throughout the world. So far anthropological studies have shown that women, like men, learn that aggressive behaviour is an appropriate expression of anger. This observation falls in line with the social learning theory, which proposes that every behaviour is learned. Several studies have suggested that as much as men learn that they can use violence on women (for various gender specific reasons), women too learn and may initiate physical aggression against their spouses, or when struck they may strike back and do so with a weapon (Gelles 1994; Farrington 1980; Strauss and Hotaling 1980).

According to Richters (1992), abuse may teach young women that the best way to beat the system is to join it and become manipulators and abusers themselves. Dobash and Dobash (1992) suggest that in every country where the issue of battering has been recognised, there are well-known cases of women in prison who have killed their male partners after years of `his violent abuse'. Jones (1980),

Browne (1987) and Daly and Wilson (1988) all concur that some women have become *causes célèbres* and are subsequently released. Others remain unknown and serve out sentences because they were first abused by their male partners and then failed by a society unwilling or unable to provide the necessary means of protection or escape.

Children's Violence Against Parents

The study found a relatively low rate of violence by children against their parents in families. Only two cases were reported during the six-month period, i.e. 2.8 per cent of the total reports made. It should be noted that, as earlier mentioned, only severe cases of domestic violence attract media attention and thus on the ground this form of domestic violence is likely to be much higher.

In most cases, children's violence against their parents is more often psychological than physical. It can be assumed that constant nagging, disobedience and disrespect amount to mental violence in that it causes mental and emotional pain; whereas such forms of violence are rarely recognised, in the extreme some children physically assault their parents causing injuries and even death. In Kenya, the latter cases have become quite common. For example, in one of the reports,

> a 50-year-old man had his head chopped off by his son following a quarrel, over food (DN, 27 March 1997).

In another incident,

> a man killed his mother after a quarrel, then hanged himself (KT, 23 April 1997).

Further research is necessary on the issue of children's violence against parents as a form of domestic violence.

Implications of Findings in International Perspective

On average, 12 severe cases of domestic violence are reported in the newspapers in a month in Kenya. This indicates the existence of a serious yet largely ignored problem. Taking into account the high levels of under-reporting in cases of domestic violence, it can be concluded that levels of domestic violence are much higher than indicated by this study.

The severity of the acts of violence executed upon women emphasises the gender-based aspects of domestic violence. Like all other historical manifestations, gender violence is embedded in the socioeconomic and political contexts of power relations between men and women. In a patriarchal social situation, male power dominates. As a result men feel mandated to violate women given their low bargaining power in family relationships. This could be one of the major explanations as to why men beat, batter and kill women.

The study also shows that women's violence against men exists, though to a lesser extent. This can be termed an emerging trend because traditionally, women were never allowed even to express anger in most Kenyan societies. There is need for research in this area too. For example, comprehensive and scholarly historical and anthropological work analysing the roles of women in child abuse, infanticide and other forms of violence has been done mainly in Europe and America (Jones 1980). These studies have also been careful to explore the cultural, situational and motivational contexts within which such violence occurs. A context-based approach has shown, for example, that when women commit acts of infanticide, these are usually `acts of desperation... principally the products of desperate circumstances' (Daly and Wilson 1988; Jones 1980). Cross-cultural evidence demonstrates that infanticide sometimes occurs because of cultural beliefs about deformed children but most commonly because of desperate material circumstances that `limit the capacity to care for the child; often because men are unwilling to assume the responsibility for parental support' (Daly and Wilson 1988). British and American research reveals that for the most part, women usually remain physically passive in order, they believe, to avoid a more serious or prolonged attack. Most women believe that attempts at self-protection or retaliation only increase the severity of an attack (Dobash and Dobash 1979; Einsberg and Micklow 1974). Concurring with earlier research, Saunders' study of a group of physically abused women in the United States shows that their violence is typically associated with self-defence, involves a narrow range of acts and is not usually intended to inflict injury (Saunders 1986).

The findings imply that children are also not safe in their family environment.

The United Nations made a promise to children when it put together `The Rights of the Child' in 1990. Article 19 asks that countries take `all appropriate legislative, administrative, social and education measures to protect the child from all forms of physical and mental violence ... maltreatment or exploitation including sexual abuse'. Whereas most countries so far have made efforts to implement prevention of child abuse and neglect in schools and public places, in Kenya the government has not taken any strategy to prevent violence against children in the home.

For example, during the 1980s, most developed countries introduced legislation and social measures aimed at giving women and children better protection against violence in intimate relationships. Less developed regions have been slow to recognise the extent of the problem in their own countries and international development agencies working on behalf of women in these countries have by and large also hesitated to take a stand on the issue of violence against women and children in the family.

Kenya, like many other countries in the world, is being faced by the reality of largely ignored social problems. Domestic violence threatens the stability of the very institution that forms the core of the society, the family.

The right to a private family life does not include the right to abuse family members. International and regional human rights instruments universally guarantee the right to a private life and to a home. The family is a private domain, a source of comfort and provides nurturance for the mutual growth of its members. The United Nations acknowledged this value by proclaiming 1994 the International Year of the Family. While the importance of the family as a societal structure cannot be underrated, excessive faith in its nurturing capacities may lead to efforts to sustain the family unit even where members are being victimised by other family members. In the face of domestic violence, the maintenance of the family as an intact unit takes precedence over the interests of the individual within it. The right to be free from domestic violence or the threat of domestic violence is a fundamental and universal human right.

Conclusions and Recommendations

Domestic violence in Kenya has emerged as a serious issue, a problem that calls for individual, local and national concern and action. So far violence within the family unit is an extremely private affair. As a result the majority of its victims continue suffering in the muffled recesses of this private domain. There is no government policy formulated to deal with the problem, neither is there an existing legal framework aimed at protecting victims and would-be victims of domestic violence.

It is noteworthy that there are certain values which legitimise a certain amount of family violence. For example, most societies condone the physical disciplining of children and women, and if they do not do so now, they have done so in the last 100 years. This explains why violence against children and women is so common-place.

Domestic violence in Kenya requires legal interventions. Legal strategies must be formulated and action taken as one of the most effective means of bringing domestic violence to an end. For example in all countries where domestic violence has emerged as a serious issue, people involved with the law have been forced to confront a central question, namely, what role, if any, the criminal justice system.

For Kenya much more information is required about the forms and conditions of domestic violence. Specifically, more information about violence against women and children is urgently needed, especially through diachronic studies tracing changes through time. This necessary information can only be collected through original research since there is no existing system of data collection on domestic violence in Kenya. And while some statistics may be available, such as records on rape, they may give a misleading picture of the real situation.

Such research will need to be funded by donor agencies because social research is seldom given high priority by the government of Kenya owing to severe financial constraints and partly because of the hidden nature of the problem. Indeed, the government may be unwilling to admit there is problem that needs to be addressed.

The Kenyan government and other agencies working in the country must recognise that violence in the home is a serious problem impeding development, as well as a human rights issue for its victims, of whom most are women. Development agencies must make clear and unambiguous statements condemning violence against women and must make it a priority to design and support programmes for eliminating it.

Consequently, programmes aimed at eliminating family violence must be aimed at men as much as or even more than at women . Until these changes occur domestic violence will remain a growing problem for Kenya.

Notes
1. *Kenya Times* (FKLT), *Daily Nation* (DN), *The East African Standard* (TES).
2. The term abuse refers to any act likely to inflict physical or mental harm such as beating, bettering, rape, incest and murder among others.
3. A panga is a long and sharp knife-like tool used for cultivation.
4. A rungu is a long, double-edged, sword-like tool which people normally keep in their homes for self defence.

3. Gender Differentials in Students' Perception and Participation in Violence: A Case Study of the University of Lagos

Funmi Bammeke*

This article identifies various forms of violence occurring in the university and distinguishes between overtly expressed forms of violence such as physical assault or rape, and covertly expressed violence such as leering, jeering, patronage, insult and sexual harassment. Its concern is that whereas the former (overt violence) is easily recognised as violence, the latter goes on unobtrusively in social relations but not without affecting the quality of life and education in an institution such as the university.

The article also argues that the different social values and roles attached to the sexes over the years affect individual's perception of the opposite sex and make the denigration of one easier than the other. It attempts to show through an exploratory study that the various forms of

* Department of Sociology, University of Lagos, Akoka, Nigeria.

The perceived legitimacy or illegitimacy of an action may also determine its categorisation as violence. In the university, students' demonstration of dissatisfaction often manifests through the disruption of classes, blockading of the institution, destruction of property and physical assault of individuals whose personae or offices symbolise the source of the grievance. Such actions are no doubt violent, but the intervention of law enforcement agents introduces the dimension of legitimacy, as the police, in their bid to restore order, perpetrate more violence. With the use of more sophisticated weapons, they often leave more people, including non-students, dead or injured, while women students may become victims of their 'protection'.[1]

Violence in the university also manifests in the largely nocturnal activities of secret cults characterised mostly by bloody and often fatal attacks on members of rival groups, physical attacks on men students and the rape of women students (Ojobo 1992). Other incidents of assault and rape not connected with secret cults also occur.

Public awareness of these overtly expressed forms of violence is high as they are often reported in the media. The rape of women students, the burning of a vice-chancellor's residence and the murder of two students were reported in identified universities by *Sunday Punch* (9 February 1997), and *The Guardian* (20 June 1997 and 23 June 1997) respectively.

While this study was going on, violence erupted right in the study setting. Inter-cult clashes claimed the life of a male year III Mechanical Engineering student, Wale

Owoade, a suspected member of Buccaneer Confraternity, one of the secret cults. The 4 September 1997 killing was still being investigated when a male Philosophy student on extra session, Akinola Akinkumi, suspected to be a member of rival cult group - Black Axe, was killed on 6 September.

Violence on campus, however, is not restricted to loss of life, infliction of bodily injury or the destruction of property. Other forms of violence found in the university include insults, leer, sneers, patronage, bullying, vocal violence and sexual harassment (Hanmer and Maynard 1987:5).

The dictionary meanings of these words have been paraphrased as follows:

Leer: To look at someone in a manner which expresses a desire to harm and/or have sexual relations with the person.

Sneer: To smile or speak mockingly.

Patronise: To treat someone condescendingly. That is, in a manner showing superiority to that person even though one makes a pretence of equality.

Bully: To oppress others by force or threats.

Insult: To offend the self-respect of someone.

(Paraphrased from *Oxford Dictionary of Current English*, 1993.)

The definition of sexual harassment as 'deliberate, or repeated, unsolicited verbal comments, gestures or physical contact of a sexual nature' (Merit Board 1981:2) also makes it a form of violent behaviour albeit covert. Although 'bloodless', these forms of violent acts are equally potent in their capacity to devalue the quality of life and education in the university (EORP 1994:3)[1] by undermining victims' self-esteem and eroding their confidence so that they do not fully realise their potential.

Generally, violence in the university, like elsewhere, is multidirectional. It could be within gender, as in men's violence to men or women's violence to women. It could also be between gender as in men's violence to women or women's violence to men. There is also a dynamism in the continuum of victimisation as victim and offender may change position even in the same context. For example, in responding to violence, a victim may be so violent as to become the offender.

Knowledge on Violence

The quest to understand violence as a phenomenon has led to an increase in its study, but very few of these studies are directed towards the understanding of violence in institutions of higher learning. Literature shows that even where studies had been conducted, they had been in relation to physical violence and rape. For example, Kathleen (1995), Warshaw (1988) and Martin and Hummer (1989) examine the incidence of rape in different universities. Ojobo (1992) also reported physical violence, assault and rape in Nigerian universities.

Covert violence, the focus of this study, is discussed pointedly in literature as sexual harassment[2], hence the need for a review of literature on this topic.

Some existing studies focussed on the workplace (Russell 1984; Smith 1994) while some are directed at covert violence specifically in the university (Kathleen 1995; EORP 1994). Others consider both the workplace and the institution of learning in their discussions (Sheffield 1987; Rhode 1989).

In spite of the different contexts of studies, similar patterns emerging in the manifestation of sexual harassment confirm that the framework used to examine sexual harassment in the workplace could also be used to organise and evaluate research on sexual harassment in educational institutions (Russell 1984:20). There is abundant evidence that the term sexual harassment is used in relation to specific contexts such as education or work environment (EORP 1994:3). Theoretical explanations on sexual harassment are based on the need to sustain the power relationships of patriarchy, the ideology of male superiority (Sheffield 1987). The review is presented under four sub-headings: Definitions, Characteristics of Victims and Perpetrators, Effects of Sexual Harassment and Gaps in Literature.

Definitions

There is no rigid definition for sexual harassment, but according to Farley (1978) the term explains forms of behaviour to which women were well acquainted before it was named. She defines sexual harassment unequivocally as 'unsolicited non-reciprocal male behaviour that asserts a woman's sex role over her function as worker' (1978:14-15).

The common definition adopted by scholars is the one used by the Merit Board in the study of sexual harassment in the federal workplace in the United States. It defines sexual harassment as 'deliberate or repeated, unsolicited, verbal comments, gestures or physical contact of a sexual nature that is considered to be unwelcome by the recipient' (1981:2). Russell (1984) and Rhode (1989) also used this definition which, unlike Farley's does not exclude the possibility that men can also be sexually harassed.

A specific definition was given by the National Advisory Council on Women's Educational Programs to cover academic sexual harassment. It defines sexual harassment as 'the use of authority to emphasise the sexuality or sexual identity of a student in a manner which prevents or impairs that student's full enjoyment of educational benefits, climate or opportunities' (Till 1980:7).

Sexual harassment in the university was described more broadly by the EORP to refer to:
> A continuum of behaviours rather than to one 'thing', ...a shorthand term for... reminding one about the connection between a (sic) event thought to be an ordinary facet of living as an urban woman—being teased by a group of young men as she walks past. A lifetime of enduring unwanted teasing and touches, bribes or threats connected with sex, insults and comments about one's physical appearance, and the constant reality of people being raped (1994:23).

The choice of words in the definition of sexual harassment in the university may create loopholes in regulations meant to discourage such behaviour. As noted by Crocker (1987), the use of words like 'inappropriate' or 'unwelcome' imply that some leers or pinches may be appropriate or welcome and therefore may not be considered as harassment. Words like 'coercion' or 'force' also imply that unforced sexual favours are acceptable, but Crocker wonders whether even unforced sexual favours are truly willingly bestowed given the powers of the professors over students. According to him, the threat of punishment ('fuck or flunk') or the promise for a reward ('A for a lay') makes little difference to the student who may not need to have the alternatives articulated in order to protect herself (Sheffield 1987:181).

Characteristics of Victims and Perpetrators

Age, marital status and sexual composition of the workplace (Russell 1984:27) are factors identified as crucial in determining who will be sexually harassed. Research findings show that men and women who are likely to be harassed are, among other things, young, unmarried and are in a workgroup composed predominantly of the opposite sex (Russell 1987; Rhode 1989). In the Merit System's Study, 42 per cent of the women and 14-15 per cent of the men reported incidents of sexual harassment. Most of the women reported that their harassers were male and most of the men reported that their harassers were female. The studies on sexual harassment in the university provided no statistics but specified that women students were victims (e.g. EORP 1994; Kathleen 1995).

Effects of Sexual Harassment

Documented effects of sexual harassment are in relation to women. The first is that women, both in employment and an academic setting find it difficult to have mentors (Rhode

1989). The second is that women do expect redress and therefore may not lodge any complaint, particularly as such complaints may be trivialised.

Rhode notes that 'male business executives generalise from their own experience and find it impossible to believe that female employees are really troubled by sexual overtures'. She quoted a respondent to a *Harvard Business Review* survey who said: 'I have never been harassed but I would welcome the opportunity (1989:232)'.

The respondent's attitude shows that gender may impact on the perception of violence because 'what men often experience as fun or flirtation, women often experience as degrading and demanding' (Rhode 1989:233).

Gaps in Literature

There is a need to enlarge the body of literature on covert violence in educational institutions, particularly because of their implications, for quality of life and academic excellence. Gaps in literature relate to forms of covert violence and the extent of victimisation and perpetration by students, staff and other members of the university community.

Classifying all covert acts as sexual harassment or using the term covert violence interchangeably with the term sexual harassment (Harlow 1996:68) is problematic. Some acts, though violent, may not be sexual in nature. A man who patronises a woman may do so because of her sex but without any 'gesture or physical contact of a sexual nature'.

Sneering at a person, insulting or bullying a person may also be violent in the sense of diminishing that person, but may be devoid of sexual overtures which would have qualified them as harassment. Rather than classify all covert violence as sexual harassment, covert violence should include sexual harassment (see Hanmer and Maynard 1987:5).

Farley's definition also rules out the possibility of men being sexually harassed, but although the victimisation rate may be extremely low for men, the incidence should not be ruled out without any empirical knowledge.

Gender Relations and Violence

A consideration of the various forms of violence on campus shows that central to them, is the attempt to control the behaviour of others. If violence is indeed 'any action or structure that diminishes another human being' (Pinthus 1982:2), then it is important that the definition of violence be widened beyond the 'use of force'.

It could be conceived of as the use of force its threat or other subtle means to compel or restrain a particular behaviour in others. This conception shows that violence is being considered in its active sense where it can manifest in physical, sexual, emotional, cognitive, verbal, visual and representational forms (Harlow 1996:3). It also means that considered through its mode of expression, active violence can be overt or covert.

The interest here is not in the overt physical assault where the actor's intention is clear and the immediate consequences of the action are observable on the victim. Rather, interest is in the various forms of overt violence, so subtle as to be almost unobtrusive to everyone but the victim, the context of which is the socially constructed relations of males and females.

Covert violence occurs in the university on a large scale but is often unreported because the onus of proof is on the victim. Students' perception also contributes to the under-reporting because although many find the various acts disturbing and unpleasant, they do not perceive them as violence. Their understanding of violence relates more to physical assault and rape: and this is as true for students as it is for most university officials and teachers. The implication of this is that a complainant is ridiculed or disbelieved as those expected to adjudicate trivialise the issue.

The central thesis here is that the incidence of covert violence illuminates gender relations among students. Men and women students are not equally affected either as victims or offenders. Women students are more likely than men students to be teased, touched suggestively or to experience sex related threats. They are also more likely to experience covert violence from their men colleagues as well as lecturers. Although lecturers may also experience covert violence from students, their social position *vis-à-vis* that of student eliminates the unarticulated threat of punishment perceived by student victims, especially women students.

Women students are also faced with a contradiction not experienced by men students. In an environment where sex is no basis for intellectual inferiority, women students have to show that their academic success does not derive from their sexuality, particularly if their dressing or general conduct is at variance with the social definition of the 'good' or 'decent' student. In the event of sexual harassment, the woman student is obliged to prove that her complaint is not just a malicious deception enacted to put her alleged offender on the defensive. Also in this case, the extent to which she is judged to be 'good' or well behaved will determine the extent to which her 'story' is believed.

On the contrary, men students do not have their intellect doubted on the basis of their sexuality. Apart from this, the social construction of femininity is such that a woman student who makes unsolicited sexual initiatives towards a man loses social sympathy and respect and is deemed to deserve the actions of her 'victim'. Unlike her, a man student who does the same thing does not experience a loss of social respect or self-esteem. This contradiction confirms that 'what men... experience as fun or flirtations, women experience as degrading and demanding' (Rhode 1989:233).

The fact of the possibility of covert violence, its threat or its allegation inhibit the full realisation of individuals' potential and (or) compromise academic excellence. To this extent, the effect of covert violence goes beyond perpetrators and victims. All members of the university community are affected as the merit system is questioned and individual competence is doubted.

It is against this background that this study was conceived, generally to facilitate an understanding of issues raised. The main objective of the study were:

- To determine gender differentials in students' perception of violence;
- To assess students' perception of the opposite sex;
- To measure the prevalence of forms of covert violence on campus;
- To determine the effect of covert violence on students;
- To identify gender differentials in students' participation in violence;
- To conscientise members of the university community on forms of behaviour capable of threatening academic excellence.

Study Setting and Methodology

The choice of the University of Lagos as the study setting was deliberate, having been informed by the researcher's position as an insider. The university comprises the following college, faculties and institute: College of Medicine and Institute of Child Health and Primary Care (both situated at the Idi-Araba Teaching Hospital site), Faculties of Arts, Business Administration, Education, Engineering, Environmental Sciences, Law, Science and the Social Sciences, the Correspondence and Open Studies Institute (COSIT) and the School of Postgraduate Studies (all situated at the Akoka Campus). The study focuses on undergraduates at the Akoka main campus for ease of accessibility and availability of students.

Inclusion of students who could only be available at particular periods of the academic session, or who would not be easily accessible, would have upset the time frame for the study. Therefore, students of the College of Medicine, Institute of Child Health, COSIT and postgraduate students were excluded from the study.

Table 1: Distribution of Respondents by Age and Gender

Age	Sex		Total
	Male	Female	
15-20	04 (06.0)	22 (30.6)	26 (18.7)
21-26	38 (56.7)	41 (56.9)	79 (56.8)
27-30	22 (32.8)	08 (11.1)	30 (21.6)
30 +	03 (04.5)	01 (01.4)	04 (02.9)
Total	67	72	139 (100)

Table 2: Distribution of Respondents by Discipline and Gender

Faculty	Sex		Total (%)
	Male	Female	
Arts	09	11	20 (14.4)
Business Administration	06	13	19 (13.7)
Education	12	08	20 (14.4)
Engineering	10	10	20 (14.4)
Environmental Sciences	05	08	13 (09.4)
Laws	10	10	20 (14.4)
Science	06	03	09 (06.5)
Social Sciences	09	09	18 (12.9)
Total	67 (48.2%)	72 (51.8%)	139 (100)

The study used data collected within the university between August and November 1997 through focus group discussions, individual interview and survey. The first type of data consists of qualitative information obtained through focus group discussions based on guidelines for conducting focus group discussion (Morgan 1996; Knodel 1993; Folch-Lyon *et al.* 1981). The in-depth discussions were built around 14 themes, including the definitions of violence, identification of predominant violent acts on campus, participation of men and women students, areas of restriction of students, the place of sexuality in violence, sexual molestation of students, causes and effect of sexual molestation on men and women, and gender relations among students.

Participation in the focus group discussions was open to students who had spent at least four semesters on campus, thus excluding freshmen and women of the short 1996/97 academic session (they are, however, part of the survey). Each group had between five and six participants. Group size was deliberately small because of the nature of the topic, which was expected to generate a high level of participant involvement. This was against the background that a small group gives each participant more time to discuss his or her views and experiences on topics in which group members are all highly involved (Morgan 1992a).

Separate focus groups were constituted for men and women students, with each group as homogeneous as possible by age, level of study and of course sex. The principal reason for using segmentation was for comparison, since gender differences is a major interest of the study. It was also expected that the more similar participant in a group were to each other the better would be the flow of discussion.

Four focus group discussions were conducted at different stages of the study. The first two group discussions conducted before the survey facilitated the observation of participants' responses to specific questions and informed the content of the questionnaires. Open-ended discussions provided an exploration of the subject and examined the prevalence of issues. Moderator involvement was minimal in terms of the management of the group dynamics in the sense that participants were allowed to be themselves. Consequently, some talked more than others but none dominated discussion. The level of control exercised by the moderator in terms of questioning was also not high enough to qualify the groups for the term 'more-structured' (Morgan 1996:144) in the sense that apart from asking questions along selected themes, the moderator did not control the direction of discussions or direct attention away from seemingly less important issues (Morgan 1992a).

The focus group, which revolved around 14 themes, had the advantage that it allowed for direct comparison of the discussions from group to group. It was allowed to dwell on areas of interest and this guarded against the possibility of sacrificing exploration for standardisation. It also allowed for a comparison of group interest. Each session lasted an average of one half-hour.

Table 3: Characteristics of Focus Group Participant

Group	Level of Study	Sex	Age			No. of Participants
			15-20	20-25	26+	
1	200	Female	1	4	-	5
2	200	Male	-	4	2	6
3	400	Male	-	2	3	5
4	400	Female	-	2	4	6

The last set of focus group studies was scheduled to be conducted after the survey in order to observe issues that might come up in the survey but had been left out of earlier group discussions. For lack of any need to reduce or increase the scope of discussions, the last two focus group discussions were conducted on the basis already identified. The number of groups was limited to four as very little new information emerged after the third group.

The second type of data obtained for the study emerged from qualitative interviewees with individuals. The interviews were 40 men and women students selected at random. The interviews conducted by four research assistants were informal and the open-ended questions concerned the individuals' perception of violence, listing of acts which in their own opinion constituted violence and acts which threatened students mostly based on their gender.

Apart from expanding the scope of the study, information from the interviews complemented other findings.

A survey conducted generated the quantitative data. While there is no highly statistical analysis of the survey data, simple tabular analysis shows the distribution of relevant variables.

The study population consisted of all undergraduates of the University of Lagos at the Akoka main campus. Using the stratified random sampling technique, the population was stratified based on the criterion of faculty yielding eight strata, as earlier stated. A simple random sample of 20 sub-samples of men and women students based on availability[4] was taken from each stratum to form a total sample of 160.

The instrument, a 32-item questionnaire, was designed to tap information on students' perception of violence, propensity to participate in violent acts, perceived threat of violence, experience of sexual harassment, perception of the opposite sex and perceived security needs among others. Most of the questions (84.4 per cent) were close-ended. A follow-up question meant to ascertain why respondents looked at students of the opposite sex in a manner which made such students uncomfortable, included two possible responses to specify.

The fact of anonymity must have encouraged respondents to answer questions on sexual harassment what would have otherwise been embarrassing. However, 21 (13 per cent) questionnaires could not be retrieved and the 139 returned now form the final sample. Table 2 shows that faculties of Arts, Education, Engineering and Law had the highest number of respondents (20 each), followed by

Business Administration (19), Social Sciences (18), Environmental Sciences (13) and Science (9). Female respondents numbered 72 (51.8 per cent) while male respondents were 67 (48.2 per cent).

RESULTS

Perception of Violence

Students' perception of violence was more in terms of physical attack of others, infliction of injury, destruction of property and loss of life. The focus groups showed that the issue of secret cults was central to students' perception of violence. This is not unconnected with the fact that the cults had been responsible for most of the violent criminal acts on campus. Renewed hostilities between rival cult groups which led to the death of two male students during the period of study further influenced students' perception of violence.

The nocturnal activities of campus secret cults may be shrouded in mystery but not so the names of these groups and the possibility of identifying their members. Names that came up consistently included Eiye Confraternity, Vikings, Pirates, Bucaneer Confraternity and Black Axe. Members of campus secret cults often intimidate others and sometimes make no effort to conceal their membership of cult groups.

Involvement in campus secret cult is higher among male students than female students, but the emergence of female secret cults has been acknowledged. Names of such groups include Daughters of Jezebel, Amazon, Black Bra and Angel. There is however no formal link between male and female cult groups. While the former's modus operandi is violence, the latter's is oppression — a term used to describe the action of women students meant to diminish other female students who do not 'belong' to their group.

Men students are more vulnerable to physical violence such as assault, partly because of their greater propensity to be involved in such violent acts but more because physical violence is the hallmark of members of cult groups who are predominantly male and with whom other men students (non-members of cults) have to reside.

Physical or overt violence is significant because of its highly visible consequences on lives and property but its prevalence is not as high as other forms. The focus groups show that whereas most students identify and live with the fear of physical violence, they actually experience more of the covert forms of violence. So pervasive are these acts that they are taken as 'normal' parts of social relations. The word 'intimidation' featured prominently and consistently as participants ranked violent acts in order of prevalence. 'verbal violence', 'spoken threat', 'bullying', 'forceful imposition of one's will on others' and 'leering' are other forms of covert violence, although these are not thought to be as 'dangerous' as physical (bodily) attack. Rape is seen as a major threat to women students, although its incidence is not as high as that of covert violence. There is no known case of a raped male, and the typical male response — 'that would not be so bad' — confirms that sometimes what women find disturbing, men find amusing.

Survey findings were similar to focus group information as a majority of respondents (77 per cent) perceived violence as physical attack on others. Table 4 shows that there was very little gender differential in students' perception of violence as a physical attack. Thirty-eight male respondents (56.7 per cent) and 38 (52.8 per cent) female defined violence as a purely physical act, and 25 males (37.3 per cent) and 27 females (37.5 per cent) included physical attack, intent to harm and treating others as inferiors in their perception of violence.

There were also similar patterns in age of respondents and their views for both sexes. The concentration of male and female respondents in the age bracket of 21-26 years was responsible for this. Table 4 also shows that respondents within the age bracket of 21-26 years constituted the majority of respondents who perceived violence as a physical attack as well as those who saw violence as including the given examples.

Violence as Social Control

Violence and the threat of it regulates the behaviour of men and women students. The accuracy with which information from one group discussion was replicated by another group and even by individual interviewees and respondents confirms violence as a social control.

Specific locations and areas on campus have been associated with violence over the years and have come to be so labelled. The 'lagoon front', 'access road' 'sports centre' and 'high rise' areas have all acquired some measure of notoriety. All 139 respondents (100 per cent) mentioned at least two of them as areas where they would not visit at night, in response to the question that they should name areas they would not go at specific period of

Table 4: Students' Perception of Violence by Gender and Age

Sex	Perception of Violence				Total
	A	B	C	D	
	Violence is a physical attack on others	Violence is the intent to harm others	Violence is treating others as inferiors	Violence includes A-C	
Male					
15-20 years	02 (05.2)	-	-	02 (08.0)	04 (06.0)
21-26	22 (58.8)	-	-	16 (64.0)	38 (36.7)
27-30	12 (31.6)	2	1	07 (28.0)	22 (32.8)
30+	02 (05.2)	-	1	-	03 (04.5)
Total	38 (56.7)	02 (03.0)	02 (03.0)	25 (37.3)	65 (100)
Female					
15-20 years	09 (23.7)	03 (75.0)	-	10 (37.0)	22 (30.6)
21-26	25 (65.8)	-	02 (66.4)	14 (52.0)	41 (56.9)
27-30	04 (10.5)	01 (25.0)	01 (33.3)	02 (07.4)	08 (32.8)
30+	-	-	-	01 (03.7)	01 (04.5)
Total	38 (52.8)	04 (05.5)	03 (04.2)	27 (37.5)	72 (100)
Total Male + Female	76 (55.4)	06 (04.3)	05 (03.6)	52 (36.7)	139

the day. There were, however, gender differentials in the nature of violence which threatened respondents. Women students harboured the fear of rape in these areas which are usually deserted and lonesome at night, unlit or poorly lit. The threat to men students was, however, that of assault.

Women students were also restricted from male halls because of the fear of rape, while men students held no such fear about female halls. Unlike men students, covert violence also served as a social control of women students. Women students were more likely to be leered at, flashed at or given looks which made them uncomfortable.

The behaviour of women students could be easily controlled by a group of men students who occupied strategic routes even when they did not say a word (44.8 per cent of male respondents (30) indicated that they did give women students 'uncomfortable' looks). Of this number, 70 per cent gave the uncomfortable look to correct the 'bad dressing' of women students, 23.3 per cent did it for fun while 6.7 per cent did not know why they did it.

The fact that men consciously give women looks meant to correct or discipline them confirms that covert violence is a mechanism for the social control of women. Women also given men uncomfortable looks, but their reasons — 'to discourage them from getting too close' or 'to show them I'm not interested' — clearly lack the undertone of discipline present in the men's reasons.

Women often encouraged men's censorship of their (women's) mode of dressing as the female focus groups almost echoed male groups in their desire to avoid being given uncomfortable looks or to be sexually harassed or raped. Their reasoning was that such women call 'undue' attention to themselves.

Sexual harassment or its fear is also a mechanism for the social control of women students. As shown above, before a women student who reports being sexually harassed can be believed, she must be seen to be above board. This is because often it is believed that women use their sexuality to enhance their academic performance when it suits them and allege harassment when it doesn't.

Fifty-seven (57.2 per cent) female respondents reported that they had been sexually harassed, and 48 of them (84.2 per cent) made no official report because of the fear of being disbelieved, to avoid further embarrassment or because they lacked confidence that reporting would yield any positive result. One respondent's comment was that 'those I will report to are not better'.

An individual's perception of the opposite sex contributed to the relations between men and women students. Thirty-six women were equally valued in society, but 31 (43 per cent) men believed that both are more valued, while 20 (29 per cent) believed that women are less valued. The fact that women were less valued in their own perception would definitely affect how they related to the opposite sex.

With regard to intelligence, 48 (66.7 per cent) females and 43 (64.2 per cent) males were of the opinion that sex does not determine a person's intelligence. However, 16 (22.2 per cent) females and 23 (34.3 per cent) males also believed that women were less intelligent than men. Only one male respondent indicated that women were more intelligent than men.

The notion that women can only excel in their traditional roles of childbearing and rearing, and not in matters of intellect, means that the woman student who excels in this area must also show evidence of having obtained such excellence on merit.

Conclusion

The focus groups revealed many of the biases held by individuals concerning men and women students. Contrary to the researcher's assumption, women students were also biassed towards those of their own sex. Having imbibed social 'expectations' they measured the behaviour of others, especially women students, against these expectations.

The group discussions also provided the researcher with a face-to-face encounter of the 'bitterness' of university students against lecturers who are believed to be guilty of favouring women students with 'undeserved' grades through monetary payment. Further research into these areas is expected to yield findings capable of helping restore dignity and academic excellence to the university.

The threat of violence can make students compromise excellence or prevent them from realising their full potential. As revealed by the focus groups, some students 'co-operate' with others in examination malpractice because of the threat of violence. As long as violence or its threat remains a mechanism for the control of others, the university will not realise its aim of academic excellence.

Notes

1. It is widely circulated among students of the University of Lagos that some women students who had taken refuge in their halls of residence during a violent uprising had been attacked and raped by men in the uniform of law enforcement agents who had gone to the halls under the guise of restoring peace.

2. Equal Opportunities Research Projects (EORP) is a brainchild of the University of Cape Town.

3. Harlow (1996:68) uses the term Sexual Harassment to refer to forms of behaviour identified in this study as covert.

4. The second semester examination for the 1996/97 session had commenced by the time the survey was conducted, and it was expected that students might not be available in terms of willingness or motivation to complete and return questionnaires.

4. Sociocultural Implications of Wife Beating Among the Yoruba in Ibadan, Nigeria

Morayo Atinmo*

The causes and effects of wife beating among the Yoruba-speaking people in Ibadan, Nigeria were the subject of this study. Five married couples were interviewed as well as two social workers and four marriage counsellors. Results showed varied causes of violence, principal among which were male dominance and lack of communication between husbands and wives. Violent reactions from five of the six female victims indicated that Yoruba women were ready to challenge the issue of male dominance and patriarchy. Although the men did not suffer as much physical injury as the women, the psychological and social effects on both perpetrators and victims were devastating. The sociocultural implications of these findings were discussed in terms of tackling the root causes and symptoms of this phenomenon through changing societal attitudes to conjugal violence.

---
* Department of Library, Archival and Information Studies, University of Ibadan, Nigeria.

Introduction

Violence against women in all its manifestations has emerged over the last decade as a matter requiring priority attention, with evidence from all over the world revealing that violence in the home, sexual assaults and sexual harassment are risks common to all women (Connors 1994:182). It is a global problem. Violent facts range from battering (beating), incest, assault and rape world-wide to female circumcision in Africa, dowry deaths in India and militarisation in the Philippines. The manifestations of violence against women simply alter their forms according to the social, economic and historical realities in which they occur.

Women are exposed to violence within and outside their homes. They suffer violence in the hands of husbands, male family heads, male neighbours, male colleagues and other males they come in contact with. This is because these males have been brought up to feel superior to their female counterparts. Thus men use violence against women to perpetuate and reinforce the gender hierarchy, to keep a woman in her place, to stifle her right to speak, come and go, to make decisions and to control her sexuality.

Wife beating in the context of this study would be defined as any act of aggression directed by a husband against his wife. It is used specifically to cover incidents of physical attacks and sexual violations such as punching, beating, choking, slapping, stabbing, throwing boiling water or acid at, which all cause physical injury and/or death. It also includes psychological or mental violence which consists of repeated verbal abuse, harassment, denigration, confinement and deprivation of physical, financial and personal resources. Such violence also takes place in the home, usually behind closed doors, but it may become public when the woman dashes out of the house or breaks out into loud crying and wailing till the neighbours cannot help but hear it.

Many Yoruba wives are beaten by their husbands, although there are no statistical figures to prove it. Some wives also beat their husbands, but the ratio of wife beaters is much higher. Wife beating is not regarded as a criminal offence in Nigeria. As Atsenuwa (1995:50) admitted, social acceptability of the conduct makes it un-condemnable. Consequently, many victims do not consider it worth reporting. This social tolerance also results in a general official apathy to domestic violence reports.

The aim of this study is to identify and enumerate the causes of wife beating among Yoruba couples in Ibadan, Oyo State, and to discuss its socio-cultural implications on all concerned husbands, wives, their children and the society in general. In Yorubaland, men are socialized into roles that spell aggression, power, masculinity, force, use of force, women are socialized to have feeble feelings – kindness, tenderness — and there is institutional support in the family to underscore these roles. In a male-dominated culture such as Yorubaland, behaviour glorifying male superiority and male dominance manifests itself in the subjugation of women, in all forms of domestic violence and in wife beating in particular.

STATEMENT OF THE PROBLEM

Wife abuse appears to be the most endemic violence against women (Meena 1997:26), but its frequency and magnitude among the Yoruba has never been established because most cases go unreported. Information on the nature and etiology of this problem is often concealed and not widely available. This is because gender violence is often under reported for myriad reasons. It is regarded as a taboo subject; besides, such family matters are private and should not be open to the public eye.

Other reasons include the fact that a man does have the right to control his wife, to be the head of the family, the boss, without being queried. This is part of the cultural nexus in which men are seen as having a natural right to control and discipline their wives. Therefore the women who are the victims of wife abuse often deny the fact to friends, neither do they seek legal redress or even call the police. Abuse over time may have cumulative physical effects, severe bruising and all round bodily soreness, accompanying emotional distress or a complete breakdown. Ultimately, women's injuries reflect the effects of aggressive masculinity, but society feels that the sanctity of marriage is more important than a woman's physical safety.

In Nigeria, the sociocultural implications of wife beating have been difficult to determine, investigate and record because of low official reporting, perhaps coupled with societal indifference. This became apparent to this researcher from a cursory observation of peoples' attitude to wife beating. They seem to find it funny, so they laugh and shy away from discussing it seriously. Female victims would rather not report their husbands, neighbours would rather not be identified as witnesses of battering situations. In the Southern states, law enforcement agents generally regard physical battery of a wife by the husband as something culturally acceptable and have an unwritten policy of non-interference in domestic matters. This fact also became more apparent to the researcher from the few reports made at the courts and welfare offices visited during the course of this investigation, compared to its common occurrence among the people. In the Northern states, it is practically impossible for a woman to lodge a criminal complaint against her husband because there is no known law or custom which does not accept as lawful 'reasonable chastisement', by a husband for the purpose of correcting his wife (Atsenuwa 1995:50-1). Victims therefore suffer in silence or else retaliate with grave consequences.

In many instances, if not checked, wife beating, leads to murder or inflicting of permanent injury on the victim. In the 1960s, there was the celebrated case of a judge in Ibadan, who pushed his wife down a staircase to her death. In a more recent case, a man attacked his wife by pouring acid on her face because she built a house without informing him and she was purportedly dating another man. From the foregoing, victims of wife beating sometimes suffer tragic consequences. This study therefore intends to investigate the causes and effects of wife beating on the victims and their perpetrators.

Research questions that would be addressed include the following: What factors provoke husbands into anger that result in wife beating? What are the dynamics of violent acts, e.g. when does it happen, what mode does it take, how intense and frequent are the attacks? Why does it happen? What effects does violence have on the perpetrators and victims, their relationship and their children? How are such violent situations resolved? Are there aspects of wife beating that are culturally specific to Nigeria or Yorubaland? Answers to these questions could help in identifying communication gaps between married couples which lead to violent interactions.

Literature Review

Mention must be made of the fact that much of the extant literature on wife beating discusses violence against women in general. Nigeria's contribution to the literature on wife beating or wife battery is not extensive because incidents of wife battery are rarely documented. Therefore it remains, as Meena described it, a hidden problem (Meena 1997:26), and an invisible issue (Battered Women, University of Western Cape 1993:23). Counts (1992a, cited in Richters 1994:75) suggested that one of the plausible reasons for this gap is fear that research on the subject might encourage women to protest traditional gender roles in marriage – including men's right to beat their wives – and that as a consequence the institution of marriage itself could be destabilized so that family life would suffer. She explained that aversion to any such destabilization is widespread. Also Gelles and Straus (1988:19) have stated: 'We believe that human beings are less fearful of violence and injury than the violation of social order.' Thus spouse abuse, seen as a potential threat to social order, is hushed up and glossed over at both the individual and societal levels. However, the literature is gradually growing. For example, in Papua New Guinea, there are now comprehensive and systematic studies of domestic violence (defined in this case to include violence against women and men in the home) (Davies 1994:2), and essays published by the United Nations Development Fund for Women (UNIFEM) of research into domestic violence that has been undertaken in various parts of the developing world (UNIFEM 1989).

This review will discuss the different perceptions of wife beating in different societies, its aetiology, effects and factors associated with its prevalence.

Wife Beating: Perceptions from Different Cultures

In some cultures, Counts (1992a) reported that wife beating is regarded as good conduct, solid gender conformity and culturally expected. The men beat their wives as a 'physical reprimand', the beating happens occasionally and causes the woman no serious or permanent injury. Where such behaviour is customary, it is viewed as unremarkable. For example, in Papua New Guinea, wife beating is so common that it is seen as a normal part of married life (Davies 1993:12). Surveys conducted by Ranck and Toft found that 57 per cent of rural women and 67 per cent of rural men accept in principle the practice of wife beating. These Pacific societies thus consider a certain level of family violence to be normal (Richters 1994:12). In Serbian villages, the peasants and their wives alike consider wife beating as the husband's right as head of the family (Richters 1994:84). In East and North Africa and in the Middle East, men may censure women for trite or serious behaviour from simply listening to love songs on the radio to suspected or detected sexual activity.

In these societies, however, Richters (1994:78) cautioned that there is a distinction between beating and battering. Wife battering resulting in severe injury, incapacity or even death, is unusual. Also society does not condone battering, and intervention from neighbours or live-in relatives occurs before beating degenerates into battering. Should it be assumed, then, that the individual female victims in these cultures subscribe to wife beating?

In western countries, the beating-battering distinction is uncommon, as all incidents referred to as wife beating are actually wife battering. By whatever name it is called, wife beating is a serious offence. For instance, in America and

Britain, assaulted wives may call the police or resort to criminal charges. Furthermore, there are service agencies, such as medical services, shelters, support groups and welfare agencies willing to provide the full range of services a battered woman may need to maintain herself and her children in a safe environment away from her husband (Davidson 1978, cited in *Silverman*, 1981:82).

In Nigeria, wife beating is both prevalent and persistent because the society subscribes to twin philosophies, first that the wife is subordinate to her husband, and secondly, owing to the acceptance of a private/public dichotomy which renders peoples' homes and family life relatively immune to social controls, interventions and sanctions (Okagbue 1996:12). Wife beating is thus regarded as a family problem to be settled in the privacy of the home. Could this public/private dichotomy be an ideological construct which is used to rationalize the continued subjugation of women? How can the effects or the sociocultural implications of wife beating be measured when the incidents are kept out of public scrutiny?

The Aetiology of Wife Beating

In those countries where violence in the home had been researched, causes were attributed to various external factors such as alcohol and drugs (Renvoize 1975), stress and role frustration, occasioned by economic and social disadvantages (British Association of Social Workers 1975) and underdevelopment (Akande 1979) through subsistence living. Straus et al. (1980) also theorised that violence is learned behaviour and cyclical. In other words, the abusive husband learned violence from his father and will probably pass it to his son.

Dobash and Dobash (1980:7) offered a second theoretical perspective which goes beyond the psychological and social, to root its cause in the structure of society. In the same way, feminists from the industrialized West went beyond this second approach to suggest that violence arises out of structural inequalities which regard men as superior to women. They warned that the societal attitude that condones such inequality may become crystallized as a cultural and societal norm (MacLeod and Saraga 1988).

Feminists argued further that the use of violence for control in marriage is perpetuated not only through the norms about a man's rights in marriage but through women's continued economic dependence on their husbands. This view is supported by Walker (1979), who explained that battered women develop a mentality of helplessness which increases because of financial dependency and responsibility for children. Bunch (1991:26) also admits that women's socioeconomic and psychological dependency makes it difficult for them to leave situations of domestic violence. Particularly in rural settings, it is physically impossible for women to leave as they literally have no place to go or the means to get away, and there are no services available to them.

This leads to the question of male dominance in husband-wife relationships. Davies (1994:18) noted that cultural, social and psychological factors are involved in understanding wife beating and that it is an extreme expression of male domination aggravated by stress. She mentioned that in societies where men are expected to be dominant (which includes most, if not all societies) men may respond to any perceived threat to their superior position by using force and violence. For example, in times of rapid social change and development, men may feel stressed and insecure and may beat their wives the more. She gave examples of wives whose husbands' violence increased with unemployment or at the period of the year when they had to pay school fees. Husbands also felt threatened by the potential independence of their working wives, so they retained control through physical dominance.

This description of men's violence against their wives came from Papua New Guinea, which has a predominantly patrilineal culture in which wives are socially, culturally and economically dependent on their husbands (as is the case for most women in the world). These aspects of male domination and female dependency are built into the social and cultural systems in such countries where a woman becomes the property of the man who marries her.

OBJECTIVES

The objectives of the study can be itemized as follows:

1) To identify and enumerate the factors that precipitate wife beating among married Yoruba couples in Ibadan.

2) To determine the frequency, mode and other dynamics of wife beating, e.g. private/public place, instrument used, etc.

3) To determine the effects of wife beating on perpetrators and victims, as perceived by them.

It is envisaged that this study will provide some preliminary baseline data that could encourage a national comprehensive study to properly address the problem and inform the development of appropriate intervention strategies geared towards curtailing wife abuse.

JUSTIFICATION

From all over the world, from all strata of society, the fight against gender violence has today become a priority commitment for women (Richters 1994:vi). Women themselves are coming forward to break the silence which has for centuries obscured the suffering of millions, either in the guise of cultural tradition or in the muffled recesses of the private domain – the family. Countries like USA, Zimbabwe, France, Brazil and the Philippines have seen the problem raised on to their political agendas both at the local and national levels.

In the USA, feminists drew public attention to issues of domestic violence such as rape, incest, wife beating and sexual harassment, and undermined the conventional thinking that defined the abuse of women as a private matter (Bart and Moran 1993:229), Feminists depicted such behaviour as criminal and thus offered a new paradigm for examining the experiences of men and women. They argued for violence to be understood as an issue of social control whereby men as a class control women as a class. This is the linchpin of female subordination.

In the UK, research on violence has developed from a theoretical perspective that is based on oppression, exploitation and the dominance of men over women in marriage and society (Dobash and Dobash 1996:7). The women's liberation movement was instrumental in directing attention to the social structures and social processes based on the subordination of women.

Present day Nigeria shows women organizing for their own welfare. There are several urban-based women's organizations such as the National Council of Women's Societies (NCWS), Women in Nigeria (WIN) and Nigerian Association of University Women (NAUW), which promote public awareness of women's issues. For instance, WIN's major objective is to combat discriminatory and sexist practices in the family, the place and the wider society. Thus Nigerian women, like their counterparts around the world, are also kicking against violence in the family, although several constraining social factors still depict gender inequalities that are a reflection of the cultural values of the society. For example, within families, there is a preference for sons, and in school texts and the media, the socialization pattern emphasizes male supremacy.

This study is expected to open women up to face and address wife beating, instead of being evasive or silent about it. Some injuries sustained by the victims, such as black eye, broken jaw/mouth, swollen face/hands, are hidden from public scrutiny and patiently tolerated. The problem also needs to be addressed to curb the rate of human wastage on women and children in particular. Some women become nervous wrecks and their children maladjusted and aggressive.

It is also necessary for the Yoruba through action studies to search for workable solutions. This preliminary study is thus well timed, especially since there is no known empirical work that has addressed the problem among the Yoruba, and given a participatory approach whereby victims and perpetrators of wife beating will be interviewed on its causes, effects and on strategies for curbing the problem.

Conceptual Framework

This study can be anchored on the male dominant role theory which asserts the supremacy of men at home. This theory hinges on patriarchal relations which insist that men are superior to women and women are inferior to men, and these ideas are passed on through socialisation. Therefore there is social differentiation rooted in the predominant mode of socialisation in society, beginning from the elementary level as family to the school system and other agencies of social interaction, e.g. the church, the school, government, all reinforcing the supremacy ideology that man is superior to woman. Children internalise the socialisation and it impacts on them. For example, a girl who deviates from the social norm and climbs a tree or fights at school is quickly reprimanded, 'it's boys who climb trees', or 'it's boys who fight at school'.

The empirical underpinning of this theory is patriarchy, which is synonymous with male supremacy. Adherence to patriarchy serves as an important factor in wife beating in that violence against women remains a means for men to exert their supremacy over them. The social structures established through patriarchy are vehicles of female subordination. Imam (1989:155) described the structures of the Nigerian society as male supremacist. This is so because, according to her, men have real power which they use to get many benefits at the expense of women. This power, she claims, is derived from gender hierarchy whereby men are defined socially as superior to women, who are then subordinated to them. As an illustration, in marital relationships, Yoruba women are expected to ensure the success of their marriage through submission to their husbands, even if they (husbands) beat them. The virtues of endurance and perseverance are extolled to the women and not to the men, tradition insisting that 'obinrin l'o ni'le', i.e., the woman is the home maker, as if it all depends on her.

Following from this patriarchal perspective, Okagbue (1996) argued for the public/private dichotomy as an ideological construct which is used to rationalize the exclusion of women from the sources and distribution of power. She said the public realm of the workplace, the law, economics, politics, intellectual and cultural life where power and authority is exercised is regarded as the natural province of men, which is properly patrolled by the law, while the private world of the home, the hearth and children is seen as the appropriate domain of women where intervention is undesirable. Thus women's problems arise from their entrapment within a socio-cultural and economic milieu which makes them vulnerable to abuses.

From these perspectives, is wife beating persistent because males are dominant and females subordinated in the Yoruba society? Is this subordination manifested in the public or private domain?

METHODOLOGY

The study was carried out in Ibadan, the capital of Oyo State, and the largest city south of the Sahara. It is the heart of Yorubaland and very cosmopolitan. Inhabitants of Ibadan may be categorized into three: academics/civil servants, people in business and commercial activities and the urban poor. The research found it convenient to choose Ibadan as the universe of study.

Pilot Test

A pilot test was undertaken to reveal the kinds of questions tolerable to both sexes. It was discovered that respondents preferred to be interviewed by people of same sex. This was after a male respondent aggressively asked the female researcher,

> 'Ti mo ba fe lu iyawo mi pa, kini tiyin nibe?'
> If I decide to beat my wife to death, how does that concern you?

but the same respondent was more co-operative with the male research assistant. Respondents were interviewed separately, wives by the female researcher and husbands by the male assistant.

Research Design

The research design used is descriptive case studies, adopting a purposive sample of married couples with known incidents of violence. The Ministry of Health and Social Welfare in Ibadan was contacted. Only one couple emanated from this source. Four marriage counsellors were also contacted. These described their perceptions on the causes of wife beating and gave reports of cases they had counselled. However, the ethics of confidentiality, imperative in counselling, prevented them from introducing live samples to us.

Two welfare officers were interviewed. Key informants were then used, who managed to get us in contact with four families where known incidents of violence had taken place. The data gathering technique was by informal, unstructured interview. Rapport was first established through identifying with the victims' problems and empathizing with them.

Three decisions were taken:

(a) To interview respondents at home to observe family life style and respondent — spouse interaction.

(b) To make an initial statement that this research dealt with family problem-solving, to defuse any feelings of embarrassment.

(c) To assure respondents of confidentiality to ensure full co-operation.

Several visits had to be paid to some families because at times some respondents were not at home. In the case of one family, the wife kept breaking down in tears, and questions could not be put to her. She had been driven out of the home and her children taken from her, so she was in great distress.

RESULTS

There were five families in all, one from the welfare office and four discovered through key informants. For the purpose of anonymity, they shall hereafter be referred to as Mr and Mrs A, B, C, D and E.

First, it was not possible to interview all subjects at home. Mr and Mrs A preferred to be interviewed 'on neutral ground's so we went to their church and had them interviewed separately, though they preferred a joint interview. Mrs B was interviewed in her office, Mr B in his car. Mrs C was interviewed at the Welfare Office, on two occasions; Mr C never showed up. Mr D and Mrs D1 were interviewed at home, but Mrs D2 in the saloon where she plaits hair. Mrs E was interviewed in the researcher's office, Mr E at home, after several visits. He was not interested because he thought we had come to apologise on his wife's behalf. Thus it was not possible to observe the interaction between couples, and none of the children was interviewed.

Table 1 shows that beating began at the early ages of these marriages, at one or two years of marriage for Mrs B, C and D1. Mrs A was beaten when her marriage was between age two and five years. In the family of Mr D, there are two wives. Mrs D1 could not remember exactly when the beating started, but she knew she had been beaten ever since she got married. Mrs D2 suffered one big beating during her sixth year of marriage. Her husband actually threatened her with a cutlass, which made her quickly pack and leave the house, but he forced her back home after two weeks.

The table also indicates that wife beating for Mrs A lasted for only three years, between their second and fifth years of marriage; for Mrs B, the beating was less frequent than before, their children intervening before their disagreement degenerated into actual physical assault; Mrs C and D1 were still being beaten. Mrs D2 believed that Mr D would never beat her again. Mrs E was under the threat of separation from her husband.

Table 1: Profile of Families

Families	Age	Education	Occupation	(1)	(2)	(3)	(4)
Mr A	50	WASC	Army driver				
Mrs A	46	NCE	School teacher	2-5	26	3	No
Mr B	42	B Sc	Businessman				
Mrs B	38	WASC	Civil servant	1	19	3	*
Mr C	29	BA	Newspaper executive				
Mrs C	27	OND	Designer/hair dresser	1	5	5	Yes
Mr D	45	Pry 6	Messenger				
Mrs D1	40	No schooling	House-wife	All the time	20	6	Yes
Mrs D2	28	Pry 4	Plaits hair	6	8	2	
Mr E	40	NCE	Teacher				
Mrs E	40	NCE	Teacher	5	16	1	Yes

Source: Research data.

Notes: (1) Marital Age at first beating; (2) Present Marital Age; (3) Number of children; (4) Does Beating Still Occur?;
* Occasionally, less frequent than before.

The educational qualification and occupational information on the respondents show that wife beating occurs among both the highly and lowly placed in society (see Table 1).

CASE STUDIES

Case 1: Mr & Mrs A

Mr and Mrs A got married in 1971. She was a grade II teacher, and he was a driver in the army. He was her brother's friend, whom she expected to take good care of her. She was better educated than her husband, and she was still aspiring to go back to school.

Mrs A is a huge woman, towering well above her husband. She is also outspoken, articulating confidently with a booming voice. Mr A, on the other hand, is quiet but assertive. He speaks in monosyllables and takes time to reflect before answering questions put to him.

Mr A is provoked to anger because of his wife's stubbornness and argumentative propensity. He insists that, as the head of the family, he must command his wife's respect and that she has no right except what he allows. She should be submissive. He beats her because she tries to usurp his role, and he cannot tolerate any woman lording it over him. He said when he had a female boss, he knew how to put her in her place because: 'No woman is superior to a man, however highly placed'.

Mrs A complained about her husband's 'moodiness'. He always assumed a grim look and was unfriendly, whereas she was amiable and had a congenial disposition. She also thought he was uncaring about her infertility and her conviction was that he resented her because five years into their marriage, she had not produced any child, and she attributed this as the reason for his short temper.

They fought regularly, at least once every month. This was more like a case of two fighting than wife beating because Mrs A fought back vehemently. As soon as her husband slapped her in the face, she quickly locked the door because 'She wanted to fight back without interference from the neighbours.

Their fights usually lasted for about 15-20 minutes. However, there was a fight which lasted about two hours. Mr A returned from work, and asked Mrs A if she had served lunch to his younger brother who was at that time living with them. This question irritated Mrs A because that brother was not the only relative living with them. She told her husband that the young man could serve himself, she was not his slave. Mr A's response was a slap in Mrs A's face. This fight went on endlessly till she pulled at Mr A's private parts. This made him stop dragging her on the floor and kicking her.

She then considered leaving him but thought better of it. She resolved to return to school for the National Certificate of Education (NCE). This took her away from home and the fighting eased off. She later found herself pregnant.

The aftermath of each fight was that Mr A refused to eat and sulked for a few days, not talking to his wife. She would spend her money cooking meals and not caring whether or not he ate them.

She sometimes sustained some injuries such as a swollen face or bruises in the knees and elbows, but nothing serious enough for hospitalization.

The fighting has ceased. The couple attribute this to their new life in Jesus Christ, and the fact that they now understand the purpose of marriage and their responsibility to each other. They iron out their differences peacefully. Their children were not yet born at the times they were fighting, so they do not know about it. Mrs A mentioned that the children complain about their daddy's 'moodiness'; that he takes life too seriously and does not wear a smile.

Case 2: Mr and Mrs B

Mr and Mrs B got married in 1978, having met at a party. He is a businessman and she is a civil servant. He travels much in business trips, which made her initially unhappy because she did not like to be alone. When he returns from his business trips, he expects to be doted on, for his wife to serve him well-prepared food on time. Sometimes the food got burnt or she was not at home on his arrival. This provoked him enough to beat her. Mrs B is quarrelsome, she is always ready for a fight and prides herself on her dexterity in keeping grudges. She said: 'I can't be easily cheated'.

He also learnt to keep malice, but at such times when they are keeping a grudge, both of them are so unhappy, they lose weight, but neither of them wants to be the first to apologise.

Their greatest fight happened in public — at a party — when she quietly accused him of infidelity. His response was to give her a tooth bite on the arm. A fight ensued and they had to leave the party with great embarrassment.

While her husband is beating her, Mrs B retaliates with verbal abuse and cursing. She said she knows he is stronger than her, but her tongue is sharper than his. So the more she abuses him, the harder he hits her.

Mr B believes that his wife's background has affected her. She was brought up by her step-mother, who was not particularly kind to her. She has no room for tenderness or soft feelings. Mr B's parents were a happy couple, and he thought he could replicate their life in his marriage, but his wife is not being co-operative. He beats her to make her conform to his wishes. He thinks she should be totally submissive to him.

The children of Mr and Mrs B intervene in their fights, pulling them apart, sometimes asking for patience on both sides.

Mrs B has thought of leaving her husband, but he is a good provider and she would rather stay with the devil she knows than one she does not know. Also she does not want children from several fathers, so she has decided to remain.

Case 3: Mr and Mrs C

This was an unmarried couple who had been cohabiting for five years, and had produced two sons, aged three years and one year respectively. She is a fashion designer who also runs a hairdressing salon. She has enough money to take care of herself, and had even paid part of her fiancé's tuition fees in the University. After graduation, it took him three years to get a job. During these years of unemployment, she fended for her fiancé and paid house rent. He finally got a good job in one of the new newspaper houses in Lagos, but now he is trying to forsake Mrs C, with his mother's encouragement.

In 1993, Mr C promised to marry his fiancée, but his mother insisted that she must get pregnant first. So she had a son in 1994 and another in 1996, yet still her 'mother-in-law' would not agree to a wedding and her fiancé dares not disobey his mother.

Mr C visits Ibadan on weekends, but these visits started getting few and far between, so 'Mrs C' complained and she got beaten. Mr C quickly apologises after beating Mrs C, explaining that he does not understand what gets into him to make him beat her.

The most violent interaction occurred sometime in September 1997 when he came home and horsewhipped her on the allegation that she had called his mother a witch (there were marks of a horsewhip on her back and thighs). She had earlier stopped complaining about his behaviour and, at the horsewhipping, she refused to cry or shout for help. This defiance infuriated him the more and he tried to strangle her.

The straw that broke the camel's back came when Mr C took the children from school, deposited them at his mother's and asked Mrs C to quit their apartment. She has vowed not to do so for the sake of her children, whom she had not set eyes on since October 1997.

Mr C, unfortunately, has not responded to two invitations issued by the Welfare Office. He will have to be subpoenaed.

Case 4: Mr and Mrs D1 and D2

This is a polygamous set up where Mr D has two wives. Mr D is a messenger and his first wife is a housewife with six children. The second wife plaits hair in a small salon close to the house and she has two children. They all live in two rooms in a house with many other tenants. One of the rooms doubles as a bedroom at night for Mrs D1 and her children, and occasionally Mr D when he chooses to spend the night there. The other room is for Mrs D2 and her children. Mr D spends most of his time there.

Mrs D1 and D2 rotate food preparation for their husband on a weekly basis. When it is Mrs D1's turn she demands 'chop money' from Mr D. This irritates him because Mrs D2 cooks for him with her hard-earned money. But Mrs D1 has many more mouths to feed – six children – and she is jobless. Instead of giving her money, her husband beats her with a broom, calling her lazy and beggarly. She receives the beating passively.

When she was pregnant with her sixth child, she got such a beating that she thought she would die. It was through the intervention of neighbours that tragedy was averted. The cause of the fracas was that she had taken much-needed money from her husband's drawer to buy food for the children. Mrs D2 was never involved in any of these beatings. Mr D showered his love on her, and she got whatever she asked of him. However, a day came when Mrs D2 cursed the children of the first wife within the hear-shot of Mr D who used a cane to beat Mrs D2. He was surprised that she fought back vehemently, so he beat her more.

Mrs D2 said she was not foolish like Mrs D1, who would not resist a man's beating. She packed up and left the house with her children. About two weeks later, Mr D dragged her back, but not before giving an assurance that he would never beat her again.

Mrs D2 denied ever cursing the children of Mrs D1. She did not like the precedent set by Mrs D1 whereby she allowed herself to be beaten without resisting it.

Mr D thought Mrs D1 had no initiative. She relied on him to supply all her financial needs when he does not earn much money. She should find a means of livelihood rather than expecting him to dole out everything, he said.

Case 5: Mr and Mrs E

Mr and Mrs E were both primary school teachers with NCE qualifications. Mr E got nominated to the Board of Primary Education in his state, and his attitude towards his wife changed dramatically. He started finding fault with her. He complained that she was disrespectful to him and rude to his mother.

He got a new car and new clothes. He came home one day and introduced a woman to his wife as his prospective wife. His wife's angry retort was sharp and instant, so Mr E slapped her on the face. Mrs E quickly found a kettle with which she bashed the head of her husband.

Mrs E took ten years to have a baby boy, who is now six years old. During the ten years of waiting, Mr E always threatened to get another wife. Now that she had a son, she did not expect him to continue with his threat.

Mrs E promised neither to leave her husband nor to allow him to marry another wife. She believes that since they struggled together, they must also enjoy his new-found wealth together. Also their marriage was peaceful until he started having girl friends. Mr E denied the fact that he had come into money. He also denied slapping his wife on the face. He said he just touched her face. Because his head was bashed, he insists that his wife is capable of murder and that she must go. She could not stop him from marrying another woman. He said as far as he was concerned, their relationship was over and she could leave but not with her only son.

Mrs E is soliciting relatives to apologise to her husband. She does not want another woman to replace her in her home.

Causal Factors

Causal factors for the families were varied (see Table 2). For Mrs C and Mrs E, the interference of a third party in their relationship precipitated problems. For Mrs C it was her mother-in-law, and for Mrs E another woman in her husband's life. In the Yoruba traditional marriage, the role of the 'significant others' is very important. They can make and unmake a marriage, depending on the interference the husband allows. For example, Mr C's mother was able to dictate the conditions of marriage to her son's fiancée, and she still forestalled the event even after her conditions had been met.

Within each family, the Table also indicates differences in causal factors. These may be summarised as lack of understanding and good communication skills which is in agreement with the opinions of the male marriage counsellors. Then enumerated major causal factors of wife beating among the Yoruba as follows: temperament, family background, lack of good communication skills, lack of maturity, extra-marital affairs (infidelity, adultery), lack of sexual harmony, delay in having children, differences in value systems, unfulfilled dreams and expectations, religious differences, financial stress and busy schedules. These may be regarded as common causes.

Table 2: Causal Factors and Other Dynamics of Wife Beating

Families		Causes	Frequency	Form	Place	Injury sustained
A	W	H Behavioural differences lack of understanding	Role reversals	Once a month at 1-5 years of marriage	Slapping on face beating on body pushing dragging	Private	Swollen face, black eye bruises on elbows and knees
B		Behavioural differences	Disparity in life expectation	5 times a year	Slapping teeth, verbal abuse cursing	Private and public	Bruises pains from teeth bite
C		Third party interference	Frustration	Often	Slapping on face beatings on body pushing dragging	Private and public	Bruises pains scars
D1	W1	Economic hardship	Laziness	Often	Caning Horsewhip	Public	Bruises pains
D2	W2	Behavioural differences	Too demanding correction	Once after 6 years of marriage	Broom verbal abuse Care slapping	Public	Swollen face
E		Infertility Infidelity	Insubordination, Stubbornness	Regularly	Slapping kettle	Public	Bruises swollen face

Source: Research data, W = wife, H = husband.

There are some unusual causes, which sometimes even baffle perpetrators. For example, there was the case of a husband who reported himself to a female counsellor for having an inexplicable urge to beat his wife, even sometimes when she had not offended him in any way. When her daughter offends, he beats the mother instead of the daughter[1].

Another unusual cause noted by a female marriage counsellor is in the use of professional or titular designations which for some wives may be higher than their husbands'. She thought it piques the man for the compte to be addressed as,

> Mr and Dr (Mrs.) or
> Mr and Professor (Mrs) or
> Mr and Deaconnes

and she has had to counsel some wives to play down their designations, at least at home. Even when the couple have some designations, showing equality of status such as

> Professor and Professor (Mrs)
> or
> Dr and Dr (Mrs)

some women still have to be careful not to offend their husbands.

There was the case of a lady professor whose friend came visiting and asked the security guard:

> Is the Professor at home?
> No, Madam, answered the security man.
> But she gave me an appointment.
> He is not at home, madam, was the polite response.

The lady professor later explained to her friend that her domestic staff did not know that she is also a professor like her husband. This may be explained by the fact that there are some traditional values which require that women should not have high aspirations, and if they do, to be humble about them, especially if they are higher than their husband's.

THE SOCIAL WORKERS

The Oyo State Ministry of Health records of complaints made for 1995 and 1996 indicated additional causes of wife beating (see Table 3).

Table 3: Reports of Complaints at Ibadan Zonal Office 1995-96

Nature of Complaint	1995	1996
Neglect	136	100
Cruelty	011	4
Provocation	028	12
Custody of Child	043	56
Ill-Treatment	010	13
Paternity dispute	050	36
Desertion	2	-
Adultery	1	4
Interference of others	6	12
Others	287	238

Cases of cruelty, provocation and ill-treatment were said to relate to wife beating. There were 49 and 29 such cases in

1995 and 1996 respectively, which represent only 16 per cent and 12 per cent of all cases reported for those two years. From these figures, it would appear that cases of wife beating are not prevalent or that they go unreported.

The role of the Social Welfare Office is palliative and ameliorative rather than judgmental, so officials try to appease both parties. When a couple goes as far as to report themselves at the police station or court, they can no longer continue as husband and wife. The Welfare Office therefore tries to find a rallying point for appeasing aggrieved couples. They listen to the aggrieved person and invite the other party, repeating the invitation several times if they are recalcitrant. However, they can subpoena if they have to.

At the interview, the officers remind wives that Yoruba culture allows men to beat women. They ask if they are submissive to their husbands, or if they think their husbands are in a position to reprove them. When answers to these questions are not straightforward or forthcoming, they ask the couple to settle their differences 'in bed'. This is their approach to bridging communication gaps between couples.

The social workers work on the premise that a wife is her husband's property, and he can use his property as he likes. If beating occurs, it is in an attempt to train the woman. Tradition also believes that 'Alawoku l'obinrin', that is, a woman's parents have trained her to an extent, but she receives the rest of her lifetime training in her husband's house. If she gets beaten in the course of this training, that is a measure of the reprimand to sharpen her life, and it should not be misconstrued as cruelty or ill-treatment.

The interesting thing here is that some women justify the beating when they think it is `well deserved', blaming themselves for `overstepping their bounds'. In these cases, causal factors may be related more to personality or character traits than factors as outlined by the marriage counsellors or Social Welfare Office.

THE EFFECTS OF WIFE BEATING

Concerning the physical, psychological and social effects of violence on women, their families and society in general, Bradley's analysis (*in* Davies 1994:13-15) showed that they are all negative and not quantifiable. However, awareness is being raised and each country is tackling the problem in its own way. For example, there are now women's police stations in Brazil, which investigate gender-specific crimes and provide psychological and legal counselling. Although many batterers still do not get prosecuted, it is now clear to law enforcement agents that Brazilians need a wholesale change of attitude towards wife battery.

In Australia, since the late 1980s there has been a nation-wide campaign to change social attitudes and awareness around the reality of domestic violence (Silard 1994:239, in Davies, *Ibid.*). Through counselling, battered women have been helped to achieve economic independence.

Among Canada's indigenous peoples, the use of what is termed a 'circle of healing' is employed to exorcise the pervasive illness of gender violence from the entire community (*Match International* 1990:11-14).

In some parts of the world, shelters for battered women have been provided, but they may not be the solution everywhere. For example, in the Zimbabwean context, official shelters are considered inappropriate (Stewart 1992); in Vietnam, the Women's Union, which rejects shelters, intervenes directly in violent domestic situations thereby focusing attention on men's behaviour (Asian and Pacific Network 1990:185). Does this call for the design of culture-specific methodologies for the effective control and/or eradication of wife beating?

Finally, we would like to describe the socio-cultural factors among the Wape, where husbands do not abuse their wives. Mitchell (in Counts 1992a) identifies a cluster of constraints which clarify this atypical situation:

- all emotions including anger are kept in control
- harmony reinforced by moral rhetoric and sanctions
- society organized to de-emphasize gender differences
- division of labour by sex
- women participate in social life
- monogamy is the norm, wife feeds husband
- women instrumental in selecting their own husbands
- men do not use alcohol
- female solidarity.

Mitchell's conclusion is that in any society where these Wape factors are present, it is difficult to conceive of a marital relationship where a husband beats, let alone batters his wife. The challenge to this study is: Is it possible to construct general patterns of sociocultural factors which can inhibit domestic gender violence?

In Nigeria, evidence that wife battering exists came from the works of Omorodion (1991), in her study of this phenomenon in Benin City. She found that the practice was very prevalent among the lower and middle classes. There were no reported cases from the elite, although this does not exclude abuse among them. Pearce (1992) also examined the issue of wife beating and found that 40 per cent of the respondents believed that husbands have the right to beat their wives, in order to discipline them, while 48 per cent did not support this idea and 12 per cent were indifferent. This indicates the need to sensitize the members of the society that husbands should not have such punitive rights over their wives. Other notable Nigerian studies on wife beating were those of Effah (1993) and Atsenuwa (1993). This present study will build on previous studies to involve perpetrators and victims of wife beating in determining the causes and effects of the practice on themselves, their relationship and on other people around them.

The physical, psychological and social effects of wife beating on the subjects of this study are presented below in tabular form.

From Tables 4 and 5, it was observed that wife beating had greater adverse physical effects on women than on men. While the women's experiences were traumatic, physically, psychologically and socially, the men, except Mr E, escaped physical injury, but not psychological disturbance (all efforts to reach Mr C were futile). Socially, the men could rely on the traditional support that allows men to beat their wives, so they did not suffer much in that regard also.

Table 4: Effects of Wife Beating on Wives

Wives	Physical	Psychological	Social
Mrs A	Bruises on elbows and knees Black eye	Thought about leaving husband but returned to school for a higher degree instead	Resented neighbourly interference so she kept away from them
Mrs B	Pain from teth bite	Discouragement Disappointment Feels alienated	Shame and Embarrassment
Mrs C	Scars and bruises all over body, especially thighs and back	Devastated Frustration Disappointment Sense of loss (of children)	Spends longer hours at work to make more money to maintain self and children
Mrs D1	Scars on body from broom beating	Helplessness	Neighbours have similar problems, so no sense of shame
Mrs D2	Body pains Swollen face	Feels alienated	Stays longer at work so contact with husband minimised
Mrs E	Swollen face	Anger Frustration Feels cheated	Determined to fight for her rights

Sources: Research data.

Discussion with the counsellors and social workers also centred on the effects of wife beating on the perpetrator, victims and their children. They explained that once a woman is beaten, she finds it difficult to forgive or believe that the man loves her. Bitterness may set in and their sexual relationship may be hampered. It sometimes leads to separation, or even divorce. She may develop an inferiority complex, losing confidence in herself. Physically, she may become weak or ill or even mad. Such women also age fast.

The man who beats his wife also suffers a sense of hopelessness, humiliation and loneliness. He may become promiscuous, going from woman to woman, and yet distrusting female-folk. He may become very unhappy and look older than his age.

Table 5: Effects of Wife Beating on Husbands

Husband	Physical	Psychological	Social
Mr A	No physical injury	Disturbed, confused, angry that his wife should be so brazen	Ashamed to discuss with friends or extended family
Mr B	No physical injury	Frustrated Driven to do the unexpected	Stays out longer sometimes
Mr C	No physical injury	Determined to exercise his prerogative	Man must show he is the boss
Mr E	Migraine	Feels bitter	Resolved to marry another wife

Source: Research data.

The children may lose confidence in their parents and feel a sense of devastation. It may affect their academic work or career, and their marriage. Some children reject marriage because of the battery of their mothers, while others get married and also beat their wives.

The experiences of the subjects of our study did not substantiate the opinions of the marriage counsellors. None of the women was ready to divorce her husband, in spite of the physical and psychological suffering and the social stigma of wife beating. Mrs A enrolled in school for another degree. Mrs B admitted that her husband was a good provider and she had decided to stick to him. Mrs C said she could not leave until she claimed her children. Mrs D1 was helpless, with nowhere to go. Mrs D2 left and was brought back. Mrs E was fighting to remain with her husband. Why did such women choose to remain in such abusive situations?

Though the men did not suffer physical injury, the psychological and social effects of wife beating on them are remarkable. For the men to admit to have been 'disturbed', 'confused' or 'driven to do the unexpected' speaks volumes. The men did not regard themselves as 'wife beaters' or 'batterers'. They thought that physical assault on their wives resulted from unguarded moments of anger, and that the beatings occurred spontaneously, not premeditatedly. As such, they were controllable.

Discussion

Several authors have attempted to provide a list of fundamental issues that underlie most marital conflicts that lead to violence or physical assaults. Frude (1991:175) described two main approaches to the explanation of this type of family violence, namely, cultural norms and attitudes, then family interaction and psychological processes.

The first approach on cultural norms and attitudes maintains that family violence is very common, and that this reflects the fact that society condones and even encourages brutality within the home as a way of maintaining the cultural status quo. Wife beating is thus seen as reflecting and supporting socially approved male dominance and patriarchy. Among the Yoruba, there is male dominance and cultural approval of wife beating, evident in such common statements as:

Oko l'olori aya'
The husband is the head of the wife
Erin o j'oko o na
She laughed so much, the husband could not beat her

Although a purposive sample of five families is rather small for generalised statements, all the husbands in this study showed evidence of male dominance regardless of educational qualification or social status. This may be the result of the socialisation process whereby Yoruba men feel superior to women in general and their wives in particular. This was evident in the statements and behaviour of the men in the study. Moreover none of them felt remorseful or regretful at such violent reactions on their part. They thought they would do it again if the need arose. As a matter of fact, only couple A have stopped beating each other, and the other couples are still at it. This raises three issues for discussion, in relation to sociocultural implications of wife beating, namely, the reactions of the wives, conflict resolution and the future of marital relationships.

THE WIVES' REACTIONS

There was a noticeable similarity in the reactions of some of the wives to their husbands' violence. Mrs A fought back physically, Mrs B used verbal abuse, Mrs C, defiance and Mrs D2 and E also responded physically. Mrs D1 is probably of the old tradition that allows men to ride them roughshod. In fighting back, the women were curtailing or limiting the dominance of their husbands over them. This may be interpreted as a show of power, evidence of the fact that women are refusing to take a subordinate position or allow gender inequality in their marriages. Passive receptivity or acquiescence of male dominance is fast giving way to sharp reactions, such as retaliation (fighting back) or moving out (separating oneself from a violent husband).

Could this be an indication of women's attempt to change the power relations within the family, albeit at the individual level? For too long, the Yoruba woman has suffered much oppression at the hands of her husband.

While acknowledging the exploitative and oppressive character of Nigerian society, Imam (1989:2) quoting Muhammad rightly observed that women are expected to make more of a commitment to marriage than men. She added that women are forced to sublimate themselves in family life because other avenues of social success are often closed to them by ideology, law and particularly custom and tradition. Imam then suggested that for the full emancipation of women to take place, a radical restructuring of Nigerian society may be necessary, with changes beginning at the level of the family. Such changes could include drastic measures such as the equitable division of domestic labour between marriage partners in terms of the everyday chores of cooking, cleaning and looking after children. Men must make sacrifices and become domesticated as part of the collective organised struggle to liberate society. To some extent, a few men are already giving their wives a helping hand in that area, but they do it in secret because of the wrath of the 'significant others' in the extended family and the ridicule of friends.

CONFLICT RESOLUTION

Marital violence reflects the way in which the family normally communicates and the way in which problematic issues are dealt with. Olson *et al.* (1983) suggested that healthy families are open in their communication, that they use negotiation often and that they have relatively few implicit rules. As far as could be gathered, communication or rational problem-solving strategies were not employed by the families in this study. Rather than discuss the problems or seek solutions, the husbands found recourse in violence or brutality, and the wives responded likewise.

I wish to suggest that lack of communication or communication breakdown was one of the major causes of the violence in these marriages. La Haye (1995:178) said that one of the most advertised problems in marriage is that of communication breakdown and that over 50 per cent of all marriages had a serious communication problem. To resolve conflicts, it was necessary for couples to communicate — to talk, listen to, understand and empathise with each other. However, communication might not come easily to conjugal relationships characterised by separate resource generation and allocation, where husbands and wives ordinarily did not pool their resources in managing their households and sharing leisure activities. This fact was stated by Adepoju (1997:57), and it is true of many Yoruba couples.

Husbands and wives keep separate accounts and wives hardly know what their husbands earn in income, and vice versa. Yet economic conflicts constitute a major area in conjugal conflicts. As Nigeria continues to experience economic stagnation, many Nigerian families go through unprecedented hardships in attempting to keep body and soul together. Conflicts do arise in families over disagreements on fund distribution for the different needs of family members. Money is in short supply and tempers are very high, especially where there are too many mouths to feed. Some spouses travel abroad in search of greener pastures, while others combine several jobs all in the bid to make financial ends meet. These measures do help to pull spouses apart as there is hardly any time left for leisure activities or mutual communication.

The Future of Marital Relationships

It was quite interesting that in spite of the beatings, the wives as well as the husbands in this study preferred to remain married to each other, except Mr E who wanted to replace his wife (this is more so, perhaps, because he thinks he has found a more suitable wife). Even Mrs C whose 'husband' has left indelible marks of his anger on her body, confessed that she would stay, not just because of her children but because she still 'loves' her husband. She believes he would be alright without his mother.

The marriage institution, i.e. that between one man and one woman, is still extremely important in this society. Unmarried people desire to get into marriage and married people desire to remain married in spite of all its frustrations. Religious institutions are very supportive of marriage and assigned roles, to husbands to be protective and providing and to wives to be supportive and reproductive.

Concerning the emancipation of women, several CBOs and NGOs have already gone to work, counselling and encouraging women towards empowerment through economic independence so that they can cope in times of crisis. These organisations also raise women's awareness to the fact that wife beating impinges on their legal and human rights and they should not take it lying down.

Much work still needs to be done, however, with regard to challenging the root causes of conjugal violence in addition to treating its symptoms. This means challenging the social attitudes and beliefs that undergird male dominance and renegotiating the meaning of gender inequities and the balance of power between men and women at all levels of society.

Note

1. The counsellor, after much probing, finally diagnosed that the man must have been under some demonic force energized by his 'oriki', or cognomen, which goes thus:

   Omo a fi 'da gbongbo
   Be ana e l'ori
   One who uses a cutlass
   To cut off his in-law's head.

   Cognomen are pet names or praise names used to greet people and give them a feeling of elation and pride in their ancestry.

5. Women and the Dialectic of War: A Comparative Study of the Portrayal of Women in the Nigerian Civil War Fiction

Augustine Uzoma Nwagbara *

Between May 1967 and January 1970, Nigeria experienced the most tragic and gruelling conflict in its history, a thirty-month civil war. Within this period, just six years after attaining independence, Nigeria engaged in a war which entailed severe acts of cruelty, suffering and disorder.

The wanton destruction of life and property that occurred at this time remains unprecedented in the country's history. The conflict raged between the defunct Biafra, situated in south-eastern Nigeria, and the Federal Government of Nigeria.

The war and the violence that followed had widespread social consequences, especially on interpersonal relations.

---
* Department of English, University of Lagos, Akoka, Lagos, Nigeria.

Remarkable in this regard is the issue of gender violence or gender related forms of violence. Though the violence was not drawn out along gender lines, gender patterns could be delineated from the forms of violence that prevailed in the war. The preoccupation of this article is to identify, outline and discuss the gender manifestations and interpretations of the Nigerian civil war. In its analysis, the article examines the relationship of violence and the civil war as it affected women by studying selected fictional writings which deal with the experiences of the Nigerian civil war.

The depiction of the Nigerian civil war in literary works, especially fiction, represents attempts to imaginatively recreate the various experiences of the war. Though not factual, these writings have turned out to be a credible way of representing realities. Ezeigbo (1991:1-2) observes:

> Situations of armed struggle give rise to imaginative literature based on the events of the conflicts. War creates a new form of reality which is different from what is understood as reality in normal times.

War situations have often resulted in great outpourings of literary creativity and other forms of imaginative work. Apart from constituting an avenue for relieving pent-up emotions, literary writings provide an opportunity for articulating ideas that ordinarily would be considered inflammatory, too subjective and sensational. It is a subtle and inoffensive medium for recreating the harsh realities and experiences of war.

Also fiction usually accounts for social reality using purely human indices such as the emotions and sensibilities of the individuals who constitute society. It explores the psychological and social circumstances of its subject matter through human consciousness. Literature, especially fiction, captures the totality of human experience as in wars and similar conflicts. While other disciplines present facts by explaining, describing and analysing them, literature 'dramatically' recreates reality through fictional characters and their actions. As a tool for studying the Nigerian civil war, who seek the trauma of the war. Thus, it constitutes an essential instrument for studying society and the individuals who people it.

LITERATURE REVIEW

Nigerian fiction written in English is a twentieth-century phenomenon, commencing in the late 1940s and/or early 1950s. Before then literature was primarily in the oral form as folktales, songs, fables and so on. In other words, Nigerian literature in English, fiction particularly, is a colonial legacy. And being an outcome of colonialism, the literature of this era primarily addressed issues of colonialism and nationalism. Evidently, most of the writings were nationalistic in orientation, expressing protests against western imperialism in Africa (Achebe 1964, 1965, 1969, 1975; Amoda 1972; Binns 1979; Ogungbesan 1979). Notable works of this generation include Achebe's *Things Fall Apart* (1958), Munnonye's *The*

Only Son (1963). Predictably, most of the works were neither gender-focused nor even gender-sensitive.

Serious gender focus in written Nigerian fiction appeared in the work of Flora Nwapa, the first female novelist and publisher (Otokunefor and Nwodo 1989). In *Efuru* and her subsequent work, Nwapa has female protagonists and entirely address the experiences of women from the traditional society up to contemporary times. Elechi Amadi's *The Concubine* is portrayal of life in an African society before European incursion into Africa (Izevbaye 1971; Nwoga 1978; Ogungbesan 1978, 1979).

The seeming lack of concern with gender issues in early Nigerian fictional writings can be traced to the fact that writers of the period were preoccupied with nationalistic and cultural issues as a means of discountenancing the negative propaganda about Africa instituted by western scholarship and other media (Achebe 1954, 1975; Emenyeonu 1972; Nwoga 1978; Taiwo 1979).

As a pioneer feminist work, *Efuru* presents an impressive portrayal of the plight of women in traditional Igbo society. The novel treats themes such as barrenness, women's empowerment and the status of women in Igbo society. In this society, women's status was defined mainly as daughters, wives and mothers (Mojola 1988, 1989).

Even after independence, not much attention was focused on women specifically in fictional works; emphasis shifted from culture and colonialism to issues of nationhood and the attendant problems of independence (Irele 1981; Izebaye 1971; Ogungbesan 1979; Innes and Lindfors 1979). This period produced a vibrant and extensive volume of literary works. Cyprian Ekwensi, a male writer, who wrote mainly about women and city life in *Jagua Nana* calls attention to the plight of women, but the work represents a frivolous female lifestyle considered unwholesome through the protagonist, *Jagua Nana*, a prostitute. The novel portrays a disoriented woman trapped in the web of city life. This image of women is compromising and merely propagates patriarchal thoughts and fantasies. Literary writings of this persuasion generally create disparaging feminist stereotypes.

The civil war constituted another significant phase in the history of Nigerian literature in relation to gender. The writings of this era addressed women and feminist concerns in a fresh light. We have in this category such works as Emecheta's *Destination Biafra*, Nwapa's *Wives at War* and *Never Again*, and Okpewho's *The Last Duty*, among others which systematically drew attention to the plight of women during the war. Though the works generally focused on the war, its execution and the portrayal of events in some of the works took into consideration female perspectives and concerns.

However, the portrayal of gender in the stories reflects serious bias in terms of distinction between male and female perspectives. That is, the patterns of portrayal can be drawn along gender lines in terms of male-author perspectives and female-author perspectives, especially their themes and communicative strategies.

SCOPE

This article considers the various thematic dimensions of conflicts arising from the Nigerian civil war and their gender implications. That is, consideration is given to how gender and conflict interrelate and the sequence of relations that emanates hereby. Attention is especially focused on the contributions of women, their responses to events and the effects of the dislodged social structure on them as well as the survival techniques they adopted to cope with the war and its accompanying violence.

To effectively undertake this study, the research will analyse the civil war writings of selected Nigerian writers with emphasis on the following:

- Chinua Achebe, *Girls at War and Other Stories*
- Cyprian Ekwensi, *Survive The Peace*
- Flora Nwapa, *Wives at War and Other Stories*
- Isidore Okpewho, *The Last Duty*
- Festus Iyayi, *Heroes*
- Buchi Emecheta, *Destination Biafra*

The consideration for selection of the writers and the texts is as follows: the first criterion is on gender representation – two female writers and four male writers. The numerical disparity is explained by the fact that there are fewer such female authors; Secondly, four of the texts have female protagonists or heroines.

The research analyses the literary and linguistic content of the texts as materials for studying the portrayal of women in Nigerian civil war in relation to the necessities of war.

METHODOLOGY

In constructing a methodological framework around which this study is based, cognisance must be taken of the fact that the six texts under examination are all based on a historical experience. As such, they represent literary responses to that historical phenomenon, the Nigerian civil war. Saueberg (1991:62) provides an explanation:

> This historical novelist wants the reader to accept [the] narrative as more truthful than a text based on the dry facts of history, claiming that the dramatic embellishments and conjecture produced by [the] novelist's imagination fills the gaps in our knowledge of the past and make it come alive. The historical novel will endeavour to present a narrative universe which is both a textual continuum and in basic agreement with history.

The novelist's intention, then, is to breathe life into history so that it comes alive in the reader's imagination, thereby enhancing the objective of emphasising perspectives and points of view either previously ignored or not properly stressed in historical, literary and other texts.

This study is undertaken by means of an in-depth analysis of the content material of the works. It will largely analyse their subject, medium, communicative and technical features. The essential goal is to determine the dimensions and perspectives of violence and its significance to gender in the works.

THEORETICAL FRAMEWORK

This work will be based on the theoretical principles of feminist criticism and discourse analysis. Discourse analysis examines the discourse strategies as communicative artefacts which portray the gender ideologies of the writers and their societies. A brief overview of these theories is provided here.

Feminist criticism is the approach to literary studies which tends to expose the way in which male dominance over females constitutes perhaps the most pervasive ideology of our culture and provides its most fundamental concept of power. This theory of literary criticism provides considerations which conceptualise literature about women in terms of women-oriented interests and concerns. That is, it sets out principles which seek to debunk the marginalised positions of women on the outskirts of literary theorising and traditions. It rather tries to provide an alternative critical canon for studying and investigating female writers and women in literary works.

In a nutshell, feminist criticism is characterised by its political commitment to the struggle against all forms of patriarchy and sexism. It thus conceptualises new currents of principles and ideas for studying works on women writers that often indulge in patriarchal stereotyping of women in literature.

The second theoretical input, discourse analysis, is concerned with language use in representing violence against women, particularly in wars. Discourse analysis considers sociocultural contexts as having implications on language explication as well as assigning more suppositions on communicative patterns. This entails an investigation of the features of language which stress its concrete living totality covering all aspects of communication (Abrams 1984).

Discourse analysis projects language study as part of society and culture, as an instrument which is responsive to its environment, not as an autonomous system. Fiske (1994:5) pointedly observes that discourse analysis

> relocates the whole process of making and using meaning from an abstracted structural system into particular historical, social and political conditions. Discourse, then, is language accented with its history of discrimination, subordination and resistance; language marked by the social conditions of its use and its users; it is politicised power-bearing language employed to extend or defend the interest of its discursive community.

He further remarks that society is multi-discursive, entailing a struggle for dominance between various discourses, which involves repressing, invalidating and marginalising competing discourses so that even discourse itself is 'a terrain of struggle' (Fiske 1994:5). Consequently, in a society which entrenched patriarchal ideology, 'the dominant prominence by marginalising feminist discourse' (Meyer 1997:15).

But literary discourse is distinctive from other discourse forms. It adopts qualitative textual analysis of stories, events and incidents in literary works in order to study society. According to Meyer (1997:13):

> Textual or discourse analysis as a methodology pays close attention to language and its usage exploring the discursive structures and rhetorical strategies of what is broadly termed the text — which could be a speech, film, television show, newspapers, photograph, book, magazine, poem, or any other social artefact imbued with meaning.

And as Teun van Dijk (1995:10) notes the methodology of textual analysis involves all levels and methods of analysis of language cognition, interaction, society and culture. The distinctiveness of literacy discourse manifests in the nature of addresser-addressee relationship; the structural, semiotic and semantic features of presentation; the figurative and suggestive nature of poetic discourse; and the uniqueness of context. Applied to literature, discourse analysis examines the discursive mechanism in terms of the topics, overall schematic forms, local meanings, style and rhetoric that come into play in the ideological reproduction and recreation within the content of literary works (van Dijk 1991; Meyer 1997).

Discourse analysis, Fiske (1994:3) claims, has three dimensions at the level of practice. These are:

> topic or area of social experience to which sense making is applied; a social position from which this sense is made and whose interest it promotes; and a repertoire of words,

images and practices by which meanings are circulated and power applied.

ANALYSIS

As a comparative feminist criticism of the depiction of women in the Nigerian civil war using the fictional writings of selected male and female novelists, this article investigates the techniques, dimensions and attitudes which these categories of writers put into their works; how they depict gender and the ways in which the writers' backgrounds inform their art and portrayal of women. Certain feminist philosophical and linguistic theories, claim that there are gender differentials in the way men and women communicate and even interpret reality. This article examines the authenticity and applicability of this claim in relation to the style used in representing women in the Nigerian civil war fictional works being studied. That is, it studies the ways in which the linguistic, expressive and aesthetic instruments employed by the writers reflect ingrained or deliberate gender bias and the perceptive distinctiveness in the behavioural patterns found between the sexes. Commenting on this, Warshay (1972:3) notes that:

> Male and female are ... social statuses for which differing value systems are prescribed and which require different behavioural orientation for their occupants. Language as socially conditioned and organised behaviour should be consonant in style with other behaviours expected from the occupants of a particular status and reflective of cultural values prescribed for that status.

This fact can be examined at two levels: the level of the writers' communicative strategies; and the level of the use of language by the characters in the stories as well as their communicative attitudes in terms of gender relations. In this regard, the analysis will demonstrate: one, the gender differentials in language use and communicative style of the writers, two, similar gender differences in the expressive skills of the characters. Warshay accounts for the male — female communicative distinctiveness using the instrumental — affective dimension theory. This states that male communicative style tends to be more aggressive and domineering as an inherent male nature, while female style is more socially oriented and shows greater consideration and love for others. Thus, Warshay (1972:8) concludes that:

> ... males tend to write with less fluency, to refer to 'the events in a verb phrase, to be time-oriented (in a particular manner), to involve themselves more in their reference to the events, to the events in their personal sphere of activity, and to refer less to others...
> Females in contrast to males, were more fluent, referred to events in a noun phrase, were less time-oriented (except where the date was the event), and tended to be less involved in their event references, and to locate the event in their interacting community, and to refer more to others.

Following this, the significance of language use and communicative style as a character delineating technique between male and female becomes cogent.

In Isidore Okpewho's *The Last Duty*, the various characters have peculiar ways of expressing themselves and in relating with one another. For example, Aku's expressive style and communicative skills contrast significantly with those of all the other characters, being the only female character in the story. The instrumental-affective dimension theory could aptly be applied to account for this distinction. Ali's authoritative and assertive proclamations; Toje's arrogant and egocentric declarations; and Oshevire's insistent and righteous convictions all portray the aggressive and domineering male nature. On the other hand, Aku's self-denying and all-involving communicative style authenticates this claim. These excerpts from the speeches of Toje and Aku demonstrate this point:

Toje

> When the Federal troops liberated this town over three years ago, the first thing that the commander wanted to know was who the elders were . Of course my name could not have been left out after that of the OTOTA of Urukpe, our big chief. When the present commander took over about two years ago, he did the same thing. They were both certain that the success of their commands here depended on their being accepted by people like me without whom this town would be nothing. I am a big man, there is no question about it, even if I have to say it over and over (*The Last Duty*, p. 5).

Aku

> I see my little boy fumbling with [what] Toje has bought him, and all I can do is shake my head. He can never know what are now ravaging my mind as I look at him. But I am glad. The sorrows I have known since they took his father are too much even for my one life. It would be a plight too sad to contemplate if these sorrows were visited on him too (*The Last Duty*, p.10)..

Apart from male and female character delineation, language and communicative techniques also project other aspects of gender differentials. This is in the biases embodied in the discourse strategies employed in the process of literary creativity. Generally, a writer can order linguistic, rhetorical and literary features in such a way that they serve as devices for subordinating women, especially in their representation. Also characters in a story can equally make use of invective and undignifying linguistic facilities to express ingrained gender biases.

In the novels being studied, this discourse tendency features prominently. The civil war being a crisis event adopts various devices and strategies to propagate violence. In the execution of war, propaganda is usually a veritable weapon, especially in the mass media and in diplomatic manoeuvres.

As a result, there is always the propensity to use information to undo and out-manoeuvre the other party by both sides in the conflict. The defectiveness of this lies basically in the expertise of either party to outmatch the other in information management and presentation, especially using it to gain sympathy to its cause in the conflict. This situation exists not at the level of the state alone, for even individuals use it to undo one another and win favours or call attention to themselves for perceived advantage. Civilian populations engage in propaganda campaigns too even at the level of interpersonal relations and social activities. In the Nigerian civil war, for instance, anybody on the Biafran side was referred to as a 'rebel', and likewise a person on the Nigerian side was considered a 'vandal' by those on the other side of the conflict.

In addition to serving the general purpose of the war at the state and the inter-personal levels, the capacity of this to inflict pain along gender lines is equally considerable, sometimes devastating to the individual who suffers it. In the novels under consideration, there are many instances in which the soldiers not only physically abused or molested women but they also violated them verbally, using insulting as well as degrading language on them to aggravate their humiliation. To appreciate the violent potentialities of language and its capacity to denigrate, one needs to understand that violence exists first in the consciousness from where it is given expression. This being the case, there is a very high tendency of the conscious perception of language to incorporate violence; language therefore has high potential for violence as it is closely linked with the human consciousness. Before the physical form of violence is perpetuated, the verbal form is likely to have been given expression. In Festus Iyayi's *Heroes*, one of the characters escaping from a battle says:

> 'The war?' and he laughed. 'The war' is like a woman, deadly. We all suffer in this war (*Heroes*, p. 99)..

Another character, a soldier, on another occasion also makes an equally degrading and disdainful remark about women. He says:

> Remember that shooting a gun is different from driving big cars and going out with women... This business requires intelligence and hard work. It takes more to shoot a gun and kill a man than it takes to sleep with your women (*Heroes*, p. 119).

Even social relations between men and women are couched in language laden with violence. In Achebe's *Girls At War*, Gladys, a female character in the story, referring to love making, asks Reginald, her chance boy friend:

> You want to shell?' she asked, and without waiting for an answer said, 'Go ahead, but don't pour in troops (*Girls At War*, p.118).

These attitudes and behavioural tendencies are indices of the militarisation of human consciousness and society at large as a result of the war. This social pattern emerges with the widespread adoption of military-style life and its attendant violent attributes into all aspects of civil society owing to the war. The militarisation of social relations impacts not only on cross-conflict relations but on intra-conflict activities as well. This implies that as far as the fate of the woman is concerned, it does not matter on which side of the conflict she belongs, she is opened to all sorts of violence, physical and symbolic, even in social relationships and spaces as far removed from the war front as the home. This situation leaves the woman a double victim of the tragedy of war. Thus, she partakes of the physical violation which the war visits on the entire population, at the same time as she suffers other devastating forms of violence occasioned by her status as a woman:

> Often defenceless against invasion, women can find that armed conflict means rape and other forms of abuse by occupying troops, as well as loss of the means of livelihood (Vickers 1993:18).

The ubiquity of death which makes most women widows, childless and susceptible to rape and physical torture in various forms, has enormous capacity for causing severe mental and emotional damage. The experiences of Aku in Okpewho's *The Last Duty* buttress this fact adequately. Also, Emecheta's *Destination Biafra* demonstrates vividly the complexities and traumas of this fact concerning women.

Another gender construct distinguishable in the works being studied concerns the biassed and discriminatory manner in which the experiences of women are often presented in relation to that of the men as well as the distinctiveness between the way the female writers and the male writers recreate or relate issues of gender in the novels being studied here. In the work authored by male writers there is the tendency to portray women in a compromising fashion or give them peripheral treatment while the men are glamorised, often to the detriment of the women.

Most of the writings authored by male writers tend to highlight male achievements and heroism, thus promoting a grandiose male image. As such the male characters are acknowledged and honoured for their roles as brave officers, administrators, national heroes, etc. Even as oppressed persons, the men are given an elaborate image, a robust humanism and an enlarged conscience. Through this, the role of the men in conflict engineering and the killings that they engage in is downplayed or recreated as acts of necessity or bravery. The military men, as commanders or as ordinary soldiers, are portrayed as fully realised individuals, with a robust identity. For instance, in *Heroes*, Sergeant Kesh Kesh and Corporal Kolawole, both ordinary soldiers, are glorified for their bravery even when they indulge in callous, bestial and demeaning acts; and in *The Last Duty*, Major Ali is the great commander.

The civilian men are grandiosely represented as well: Oshevire comes back from detention exonerated and exalted; Osime in *Heroes* is almost defied for his courage and selflessness for his quixotic journey to rescue his girl friend, Ndudi, and her family who are caught up in the war. Also, Reginald Okonkwo in *Girls At War* is distinguished for his moral sensitivity, fair play and humanness even when he engages in frivolous activities.

On the other hand, the female characters are mainly portrayed as weak, effeminate and lacking in moral integrity and will-power irrespective of their peculiar predicaments and vulnerability in the war. Aku in *The Last Duty* is a classic example of this kind of negative portrayal. Her depiction as indecisive, uncritical and sexually weak underscores her plight as an intimidated and unprotected person. The fact that her husband is detained and she is socially ostracised because of 'rebel' parentage is ignored. This kind of depiction is insensitive to the fact that, as a woman, Aku was fighting several 'wars' hinged around her sexuality and the peculiar disadvantage of being a woman in a war situation. Toje's schemes resulting in the detention of Oshevire, Aku's husband; his manipulations to sexually exploit her under the disguise of magnanimity, and the hostility of the community towards Aku reveal the precariousness of her situation. In addition, Aku's son, Oghenovo, is materially unprovided for and insecure, and looks up to her for his upkeep and safety. Given this, one can understand the degree of misery Aku experiences in the circumstances. Taking Aku's experience as a microcosm, one can understand the tragedy of being a woman in any war.

Apparently, this pattern of depiction is also evident in Achebe's *Girls At War*. Gladys at the beginning of the war was depicted as quite idealistic, charming and aglow with the embers of nationalism, but as the war progressed she degenerates into opportunistic and carefree materialism as a survival strategy. She becomes morally depraved and vain. However, at the symbolic level, Gladys's characterisation represents the debasement and abrasion of the zeal and idealism with which the war started. In her downfall we see the decay of a dream and the setting in of despondency.

In all these examples, the women merely have a shadow existence, acting as foils to highlight the sagacity and prominence of the male characters. This is revealed in the relationship between Gladys and Reginald in *Girls At War*; Oshevire and Aku in *The Last Duty*; and Osime and Salome in *Heroes*. Cyprian Ekwensi's *Survive The Peace* equally gives a picturesque depiction of the image of the woman as a deprived and pitiable being.

The female writers, in contrast, present a different picture of women's experiences in the war. Their writings give a fresh perspective to the fictional accounts of social realities as they relate to women on both sides of the conflict. The incidents recreated in their works generally debunk the jaundiced picture of women as effeminate, opportunistic, vainglorious and fun-seeking, but rather show them as distinguished individuals who constructively participate in shaping the realities of their societies in the new social dispensation occasioned by the civil war. They equally highlight the ordeals of women in the war as a re-enactment and orchestration of patriarchal domination of women. In fact this argument represents a major thematic strand in *Destination Biafra*: that the civil war is a consequence of male greed, egocentricism and senseless power play. This is substantiated in the portrayal of Saka Momoh and Chijiokee Abodi, leaders of Nigeria and Biafra respectively, who headlock in a fatalistic power show which plunges the entire country into a needless bloodbath. Even as the war rages, recording a very high death toll, both men do not budge but stubbornly insist on the propriety of their convictions and are consequently insensitive to the plight of the generality of the citizens.

Generally, by systematically recreating women's role and experiences in the Nigerian civil war, the female writers are attempting a deconstruction of the subordinate social perceptions of women. This is achieved by the portrayal of women in the texts as capable of playing roles traditionally 'tabooed' for them. Buchi Emecheta's *Destination Biafra* is particularly artful in this regard. It is a decontructionist recreation through feminist perspectives of women, their capabilities and identity in Nigerian civil war fiction.

The text presents a different norm by which the assessment of gender roles can be undertaken and through it questions the validity of the gender status quo. Using the social realities of the civil war and its immediate implications in upsetting the social order, the text recreates the perceptions of man and woman. Given that conflict situations bring about radical transformations in the social system (Boulding 1966 cited in Safilies-Rottschild 1972; Holter 1972), the female characters in the texts effectively assume social positions that were hitherto male preserves. Evidence of this lies in the fact that women are at the headship of most homes described in the text. For instance, there is a marked absence of men in many of the episodes in *Destination Biafra*, and the women struggle against the odds all by themselves and confront the difficulties and challenges the war imposes on them. But the most outstanding portrayal is in the protagonist of the novel, Debbie, who takes up a career in the army as an officer, which is traditionally constructed as a male role. Even as the war begins, Debbie decides to work for peace by liaising between the leaders in the conflicting forces. They turn out to be the sacrificial lambs as they realise at the end of the war that their ideals have long been betrayed by those who championed them.

The experience of the women as they sojourn to the 'safety' of their homelands encapsulates and dramatises the totality and capability of patriarchal arrogance, especially in crisis situations. Also evident is the degree of violence to which women are subjected by patriarchal institutions. Equally highlighted here are the bestiality, inhumanity and injustice of war, which subjects women to various forms of indignity and depravity.

Emecheta's *Destination Biafra* is remarkable for its recreation of women. Unlike many other fictional accounts of the civil war, this novel does not picture the plight of women apologetically. Rather, it shows the women taking their fate in their hands by showing them as people who are capable of managing the affairs of their lives. Rather than appear helpless and succumb to fate, the women in *Destination Biafra* confront the challenges with hope and determination. Essentially, the characters are rounded and strong-minded, charismatic and purposeful. Debbie generally adopts an existentialist lifestyle full of warmth and grandeur. Her rejection of the traditional notions and roles or womanhood, and her quest for self-fulfilment express an emancipated consciousness. Through her sensibilities, a dignified image of womanhood is symbolised. She also signifies the rejection of the retrogressiveness of decadent social systems. Buchi

Emecheta in this novel deconstructs the perception of woman as dependent and helpless, especially in times of crisis. The novel thus debunks the notion of survivalist opportunism that characterised the portrayal of women in the other civil war creative writings examined in this article.

The journey motif which runs through the narrative structure of the text represents a symbolic sojourn towards self discovery and identity quest. To Debbie and the other women, it is an expedition into inner self-perception and to develop a feeling of transcendental individualism.

Other forms of women's contributions to war efforts highlighted in the texts include civil support programmes such as lobby groups for peace, establishment of humanitarian associations to assist in the supply of essential facilities, negotiation teams and other diplomatic activities. Flora Nwapa's *Wives At War* highlights some of the efforts made by women in this respect. The stories in this anthology recreate the concrete efforts of women in the war, individually and collectively, at the level of the state and in informal set-ups. The role of women in the war, often undermined in several accounts of the Nigerian civil war literature, in the works authored by women show a remarkable concern in the recreation of their experiences. Their writings and the patterns of representation of women largely conform with 'the crisis theory of women's equality' (Hostler 1972), which explains sex role change. The theory states:

Rapid modernisation as well as war and crisis often seem to bring women into 'male' positions at least for some time (Boulding 1966), a fact which may be interpreted as a national mobilisation of all resources, even secondary ones. In times of crisis the economic and military demands may, at least temporarily, lead to a breakdown of cultural norms and ideals pertaining to men's and women's tasks (Safilios-Rothschild 1972: 332).

It is from this perspective that literature as imaginative recreating of social realism becomes validated, and the texts being studied can be a corroboration of history, a social evidence.

Symbolism: The Image of the Female Body in War

A predominant device of literary communication is symbolism. It is indeed one of the methods by which literature perceives and organises experience and invests meaning in them. As Hunter College Women's Collective (1983: 24) notes:

> A symbol, such as a word, a colour, or an object, is used arbitrarily to represent something else... There can be private symbols as representations that individuals make to themselves in their own dreams and fantasies.

The prominence of symbolism as a literary ingredient lies in its subliminal attributes and communicative subtleties. Given its tendency to represent reality through the medium of symbols and imagery, literature tends to classify ideas, events and objects in the world into symbolic constructs. Thus, the perception of men and women in literature in a particular society is shaped largely by the society's symbolic constructs of 'feminity' and 'masculinity'. This, however, entails a taxonomic outlining of personality features and physical shapes of these constructs to focus on and emphasize. Though the relationship between the symbols and their representations may be arbitrary, people tend to interpret reality according to symbolic perceptions and notions.

The female body is often a central object of symbolic constructions in many societies, literary writings and artistic works. Many myths, tales, fantasies and folklore are usually woven around the female body. It is often used in expressing both sublime and mundane ideas. However, an inexplicable degree of ambivalence surrounds the various perceptions and interpretations of these constructions, and thus men's attitude to the female body. In other words, the female body turns into an enigmatic object which attracts a lot of curiosity, anxiety, concern and activity. In crisis, the ambivalence heightens so that the female body becomes both an object of veneration and contempt. On the one hand it is treated with reverence and on the other it is the object of discontent and antagonism. This paradox is captured in most fictional recreations of the Nigerian civil war and also provides a platform upon which the experiences of women in the war can be analysed. This is necessary because through it the dynamics of conflict and its relationship to gender are dramatised. It enables us to understand why women are the targets of severe forms of violence in conflict situations.

In the texts being studied the female body is the object of attack /within and between conflicting territories. The plight of the woman is invariably the same with all conflicting forces. In Nigerian civil war fiction, the female body elicited the same responses and treatment from the Biafran as with the Federal forces and civilians. Symbolically, in terms of reactions to the female body two wars were going on at the same time: on the one hand was a civil war and on the other was a gender war. Significantly, the gender conflict centred on female sexuality, the object of conquest. This gender dimension of the conflict brings to the fore another aspect of conflict aggregation in the war as female sexuality turns into an object rivalry and the centre point of conflict. This concept features prominently in all the accounts of the Nigerian civil war under survey here. Okpewho's *The Last Duty* captures this in the conflict triangle between Toje, Odibo and Oshevire over the control of Aku's body. This relationship captures the tragic consequences of the gender dimensions of the war. Iyayi's *Heroes* represent this conflict around Ndudi whose sexuality could be said to be the symbol of the ideals of unity upon which the war is dramatised in the bestial violation of femininity in the war. Osime's quest to save her is driven by his love for her while the soldiers' violence of her sexuality captures the rapacious hypocrisy of the ideals of the war: the unification of Nigeria. In Buchi Emecheta's *Destination Biafra* the female body is treated as the object of hatred and animosity upon which the anger and sentiments of the war are expressed. So the soldiers and even civilians work out their animosities on it as an avenue for prosecuting the war, giving vent to their anger and, of course, for self-aggrandisement. In fact, the control of the female body becomes a common drive for people's action and war schemes. This drive inevitably ends up in the violation of the woman's sexuality, dignity and integrity. The ultimate implication is that, in the texts, the female body is portrayed as the object of entertainment and self-aggrandisement for the men; and a source of exploitation, discrimination and fear for the women.

CONCLUSION

This study of women and the dialectic of war in Nigerian civil war fiction has explored the subject by analysing the ways in which women have been depicted in selected fictional texts. The analysis revealed that there were disparities in the depiction of women by male and female authors. While the female writers are sympathetic and in-depth in recreating the totality of woman's experiences, the male writers' are stereotypical and portray women as opportunistic, weak and lacking sufficient will-power. Also, the female writers tend to have a more comprehensive notion of the plight of women in the war narratives, and their works highlight the subtle and overt forms of violence during the war than the men whose attention was more on the basic issues of the war, namely, its political and military concerns.

Significantly, this article explored the symbol of the female body as a medium for grappling with and configuring the dynamics of gender-related violence in

Nigerian civil war fiction. It also provided the basis for understanding the plight of women and the totality of their experience in war accounts and the attitudes of men to women in situations of war.

One of the issues revealed in this direction is the notion that apart from the general situation of violence that war occasions, there are other forms of war-related violence that are particularly directed at women. Exploring the symbolism of the female body provides a more viable impetus for interrogating the issue by gender.

The use of language and various literary devices in exploring women and the dialectic of war enlivened the creative and aesthetic potentials of the narratives and realistic recreation as fictional accounts of historical experiences. One of the ways in which this is realised is in character delineation, individually and along gender lines. Also through language the texts being studied capture the dynamics of war, especially the militarisation of civil society in a war situation. Language in this aspect becomes a viable communicative medium, not only in respect of the portrayal of the war, but equally as an instrument of repression, propaganda and violence.

6. Aspects of Gender Violence in Urban Market Gardening in Metropolitan Lagos, Nigeria

Emmanuel E. Adjekophori*

Many African cities are experiencing considerable high-level urbanisation, as evident in the uneven processes of spatial growth in the last three decades. The 'unsustainable' growth of these cities along with their management problems have continued to be a worrisome phenomenon. Among these problems is the challenge to sustainable town food production. Given the importance of urban food production to the overall economy, the issue of food production becomes crucial because a lot of food is needed on a sustainable basis to run the cities.

In an effort to gain insight and understanding into aspect of urban food production, gender violence and obstacles that the low-income poor urban confront in urban farming, a neighbourhood-level qualitative sample survey was carried out in Metropolitan Lagos, Nigeria. The survey not only identified aspects of gender violence, it also examined the nexus of socio-cultural, economic and urbanisation realities that impact on women's effective

---
* Department of Geography and Regional Planning, Lagos State University, Ojo, Nigeria

participation and presents the common theme that averages the gender differentials. The study locates the vantage positions of men with access to major resources at land, information, and capital, among others, as instruments most used to subjugate females in the business of urban market gardening.

These findings also reveal that far-reaching gender conflicts are a common phenomenon and that they emanate from a mix of factors, the knowledge of which can add considerable evidence to the body of urban literature in Nigeria.

INTRODUCTION

The Istanbul conference of June 1996 and that of the Rio 1992 Earth Summit underscored a new constellation of factors which countries need to bear in mind in confronting the challenges presented by urban settlements and environmental conditions. Particularly noteworthy as part of this challenge is the issue of sustainable urban food production.

Cities are the major catalyst of growth in most African nations, and as the population is expanding at a very high rate (more than 6 per cent annually), the need for food security cannot be underestimated. Between 1956 and 1990 alone, the total population of the African continent increased from 224 million to 633 million. Over the same period, the population living in urban areas rose from 33 million to 229 million. The number of those living in cities with populations of more than one million rose from 3 million to 59 million. Clearly put, the population of the African continent had not only become increasingly urbanized but had a significant proportion of the population gravitating to the large cities, with Lagos, for example, having a megacity status (Mabogunje 1996). The excess of labour resulting from natural and in-migration, and which is unable to get into the formal employment sector constitute most significant challenge for African societies. The concentration of these groups has created a large number of the urban poor which, according to Aina (1990), includes those females engaged in farming, hair dressing, petty trading, and so on who are put into subordination by the male gender. According to the World Bank (1990:30-31):

> The urban poor, typically housed in slums or squatter settlements, often have to contend with appalling overcrowding, constant harassment, threat, forcible eviction... women face all manner of cultural, social, legal and economic problems, are made to work longer hours and, when they are paid at all, they settle for lower wages.

In many other countries, the poorest now include large numbers of single-mother households. These diverse manifestations of the phenomenon of urban poverty (which may be synonymous with the informal sector) have become increasingly an issue of our time.

The increasing concentration of human populations in large cities brings with it associated gender conflicts and violence in various fields of endeavour including neighbourhood-based farming. In sum, the problem of urban violence and poverty constitutes a major challenge in human settlement in Africa. In confronting this challenge and that of growth and sustainability, the informal sector economy cannot be ignored. This is consequently the position in which urban farming is situated as a coping strategy, especially for the urban poor and indeed poor urban women.

CURRENT SITUATION AND CONCEPTUAL ANALYSIS

Even in the most optimistic development scenario, the problem of gender violence is anticipated to prevail in most if not all developing countries during the rest of this century and may be beyond. In this context, a continuous search is being made for a gender-aware understanding and for opportunities to improve the efficiencies in operations and services at the local level, to say the least.

To date, much literature on urbanization and environment has tended to ignore gender violence by looking at the low end of the performance curve. Most of such investigations have been hinged on the feelings of men about these development issues and have not been able to provide the much-needed baseline for gender analysis. Also, research designs are often biased, and pay scant attention to the position of women in Nigeria, especially in the emerging informal sector economy such as urban farming.

Urban farming is now an omnipresent and complex feature in the urban landscape and the socioeconomic and spatial reality in Africa. It includes aqua culture, orchards and various staple crops. It is being carried out in open spaces, river banks, coastal bays, basements, rooftops, flood-plains, steep slopes, roadsides, and so on (Smit and

Nasr 1992; Van der Bliek 1992:10). While it involves people from all income groups and both genders, it represents one of the single most important survival strategies for the urban poor. Factors promoting its development include: deteriorating national economies (depressed wages, rising food prices and crises, reduced food imports), lack of accommodating land use policies and controls, unemployment and cheap labour, availability of technical and material input, and proximity to market (Mosha 1994:84).

According to the International Labour Organization (1972), urban farming is virtually excluded from the definition of the informal sector in the characteristics of African cities. Yet its contribution to the urban economy through the informal sector cannot be underestimated. The near exclusion of urban farming from the informal sector is a fact even though it shares a number of characteristics with other elements of the informal sector. These include ease of entry; reliance on indigenous resources; small- scale, labour-intensive and adapted technology; lack of formal training and unregulated markets. This is the context in which urban agriculture and associated gender violence is set and conceptualized for this study.

FORMULATION OF THE PROBLEM

The urban food production approach to sustainable in-town food transactions is an impressive reaction to aspects of the urban food problem with associated gender violence. This is especially pronounced among the urban poor and those with marginal income in their bid to respond sensitively to food problems. However, since the approach has been set in the context of urbanization, it requires a focus on urban food questions, also along gender lines. This scenario throws up related questions on urbanization, farming activities and violence, which may be crucial in comprehending the urban production.

Over the years, there has been relentless urban expansion in metropolitan Lagos (as documented by Adalemo 1991; Aina 1991, 1994; Ahonsi 1992, 1995), which is a product of increasing population gravitation coupled with ineffective urban administration and shrinking municipal financial resources in the face of increasing development needs. These factors often lead to unsustainable living patterns, hence the growth of the phenomenon of urban farming and market gardening as one of the strategies to cope with surviving the worsening situation in the city.

Urban farming, which hitherto has been overlooked by most municipal authorities, has continued to be a prominent coping mechanism with the increasing poverty confronting most African cities and Lagos included. Interestingly, the contributions of urban farming to the economy of the most urban household are no longer in doubt (Lee-Smith 1993; Rakodi 1988; Mosha 1994; Lee-Smith *et al*. 1987). What is unclear has been the content, perspectives and characterization of its operation and practice. The vexing issue of competition for urban land and its resource exploitation continues, to be a worrisome issue and is a potential avenue for gender conflict and violence in which the survival of the fittest holds sway. In most of these contests, men's abrasive approach tends to prevail with patriarchal might. They render and mete out far-reaching violence on the female folk. Interestingly, as other direction of gender violence is from men to men, or women to women. These forms are also widespread, and frightening to a level that all sorts of structural and symbolic violence are observed. The perpetration of violence between and among the genders present the most precarious situations to cope effectively with aspects of market gardening operations, which is generally believed to be the 'legitimate' business of women. From the foregoing, a persistent belief is that gender violence is mostly women-focused, whereas both men and women are violated. This is the context in which the presentation from this article sheds more light on the urbanization-gender-violence nexus.

Objective and Context of the Study

In addition to capturing the critical role of gender in the context of urban market gardening and associated conflict and violence, the study examined specific problems and espoused the various factors at play that made 'women' vulnerable to the violence confronting them in the urban environment.

Specifically, the study attempted to:

(1) Investigate and compare the extent to which women have effectively been involved in urban market activities.

(2) Document neighborhood characteristics that encourage or discourage gender relations in urban farming.

(3) Examine aspects of the spatial pattern and dimension of violence, their perception, nature and levels as they impact on sustainable food production.

(4) Examine (new) mechanisms by which urban woman cope with violence and the deprivation element of their 'legitimate' sources of livelihood.

(5) Examine the implications of (1) to (4) above on policy instruments that will improve the context of urban farming and gender issues involved.

THE STUDY SETTING IN RELATION TO GENDER VIOLENCE

The study was set in Iyana-Oba, Ojo neighbourhood in Metropolitan Lagos, Nigeria, an area with a long history of market gardening activities. In terms of geographical elements, the region is situated in a fairly large peri-urban fringe of metropolitan Lagos. It lies within 6° 5N of the Equator and 3° 1/4E of the Greenwich Meridian. The relief of the area is more or less flat as it lies on a low region with a general elevation of about one hundred feet above sea level. It has an average rainfall of 72 inches a year, with average humidity of 73 per cent. Farming activities are wide-spread, and market gardening in particular is intensive and extensively practised in the neighbourhood. Farmers trade their produce at the periodic and night daily markets scattered over the region. In fact, within the metropolis the region seems to dominate the urban market gardening scene.

As a result of the fringe location and availability of space for physical expansion, the region has been the destination point of migrant (farmers) over the years and has formed the eastern axial physical expansion of the city towards the Badagry Expressway, which again makes the study area very accessible in terms of transportation. In the last ten years the region has been receiving a large number of people with different ethnic affiliations and service activities. Foremost of these are the location of the Lagos Trade Fair Complex, Lagos State University and shopping complex, several commercial health and manufacturing centres. Using the figures of the 1991 National Population Census (NPC 1992), the region, until it was demarcated into two local councils, was as recently as 1992 the most populous local government in Nigeria.

Research Methodology

The methodological approach was to do a qualitative survey. This, mixed with the gender violence elements, emphasized the humanistic orientation derived from the interpretative processes of gender relations. Furthermore, the above was used to explain the processes that give individuals choice and why they take associated actions that impact on gender relations. This approach seemed most suitable for this study because the structure combines and taps relevant information using the levels of Neidhordt (1996) interactions, namely, the physical level; neighbourhood/community level; and facilitation level. The interviews were thus flexible and open-ended to enable informants and interviewees to define, identify and classify elements of gender violence known to them and suggest how these impacted on their perception, practices and farming outcomes.

Interviews were conducted in person, first, on a one-to-one basis by a knowledgeable interviewer using interview guides. The people selected for interview were chosen on their knowledge of the neighbourhood, farming practices, behavioural patterns, outcomes and their language ability in relation to their willingness to talk. These were people with over three years of interaction with this farming enclave, identified to be active operators. Interviews were conducted in English (Pidgin English), Yoruba and Hausa. The field interviewer was initially provided with conceptual foundations of the study and with intensive supervision from the author, who reviewed all the completed interview transcriptions prior to data entry.

Generally, two groups of individual were targeted. These were farmers (the majority of whom are male) and product buyers (the majority of whom are female). Individual discussion using interview guides was conducted in the field. Discussion with individuals and group visits in the neighbourhood helped a great deal to clarify some of the points. A checklist was used to capture as much information as possible about the market gardening business.

The operators were individually interviewed on the farm either as buyers or sellers. Selected informants/ interviewees were all knowledgeable about the subject matter and their lived experiences. They were also willing, to talk and, because of their various perspectives, a wide range of viewpoints was rendered. The interviews took place in two phases, first between January and April and then August to November 1997. Interviews were conducted between 8a.m. to 6p.m. on weekdays and weekends. This choice enabled all the categories of operators to be reached (landowners, farmers, buyers, labourers). It was restricted to urban farmers (vegetable production) since this is the dominant farming group in this neighbourhood.

Furthermore the range of questions included household composition and structure, ethnicity, state of origin, age, income level, tenure relations, status of operation, and why they engaged in the urban farming business. Specific interest was shown in the various operations, associated conflict and violence, the construction of gender relations, the problem of confronting their operations and probable and actionable solutions to the identified problems. The study also adapted Seidman's (1991) approach, which advocates establishing contextual interviewing, using two-step interview processes with each informant and interviewees. The first effort established rapport, background information and the role of urban food production in people's lives. Questions posed were broad enough for exploring the symbolic and structural violence observed and the interpretation the informants ascribed to food production issues in areas of their homes and neighbourhood. In part, the set of questions was able to (de)construct aspects of symbolic understanding of gender related violence. The second group of questions expanded on the role and aspects of gender violence and its impact on the lives of operators. This specifically questioned their ideas on aspects of urbanization, environment, informal sector economy, conflicts and violence.

The methodological approach was to develop a violence profile and identify common, neighbourhood and city-specific elements of gender relations that contribute to aspects of understanding the nexus of urbanization, farming and gender violence. The patterns and characteristics that emerged were used to present the analysis in terms of ranking and scaling the range of violence/conflicts in order of severity, defining control over various aspects of urban farming and food security issues.

Conceptual and Theoretical Considerations

In this study, the following conceptual issues are critical: 'gender', 'violence', 'urbanization', 'urban economy' 'urban farming/market gardening', 'metropolitization' and 'land tenure'.

Cender is seen here as the socially constructed, defined and enforced 'codes' and 'practices' among males and females, their roles and, responsibilities as well as societal ethics and expectations over time and across space. It refers to the societal correlates that translate into male and female inequity in social justice, an attribute that places more and more 'value' on the men to the detriment of the female, which is the outcome of male domination and female subordination. These socially constructed 'codes' (un)consciously impact on resource allocations at various levels of societal undertakings, with associated diversity of practices that dehumanize the womenfolk. It is generally used to depict and reflect women's social position relative to that of men in the society. According to Scott (n.d.), gender refers to the constitutive elements of social relationships based on perceived differences between the sexes, and acts as a primary field within which power is articulated.

In its simplest usage, gender is often misconstrued as a synonym for 'women' as a way of delimiting the social roles assigned to (wo)men. Gender is a socially constructed role that builds on or ignores biological sex. It is what categorizes a woman as a woman and defines her role (Awe 1993). This is conceptualized as a relationship of inequality between men and women. Furthermore, the gender situation in Nigerian society is a patriarchal structure which seems to be restrictive and repressive of women in a variety of ways. According to Awe (1993), women are often treated and regarded as second-class citizens, basically resulting from the male child preference which is also used to defire women's sexuality. Interestingly, this vantage position of the male gender encourages them to have access to many resources which enhance the quality of their life. For the female folk, the reverse is the case. This situation often delimits or undermines women's effective participation in development.

The urban informal economy refers to the group of income-generating opportunities and activities which urban migrants engaged in (Hart 1973). Thus, the operation of urban farming is located in the informal sector as a coping mechanism resulting from the migrants' inability to gain access into the formal sector. Thus urban market gardening is conceptualized as the range of activities which culminate in the production and marketing of garden products like vegetables, lettuce or tomatoes. The importance of urban marketing cannot be emphasized the more as it constitutes one of the single most used means of coping with urban unemployment. Throughout, it has continued to be seen as the reintroduction of aspects of rural to the urban context. The emergence of the urban informal economy is thus closely linked with women's activities. Onibokun (1990), for example, provided an account of the increasing and burgeoning informal sector in West Africa cities which is conspicuously a challenging phenomenon in the sub-region.

Conversely, the processes of urbanization and metropolitanization and their attendant constraints all combine to edge out the female gender. Land tenure as used in this study refers to the concerns of 'rights', the rights which are held in land transactions. The examination of these rights and the nature of origin and their operation, according to the Food and Agriculture Organization (FAO) (1989), are brought to bear for understanding aspects of gender violence. This is related to a multitude of other matters plus the concerns of land clearance, preparation, planting, harvesting and marketing operations.

Violence is here conceptualized as acts, activities and processes accompanying the use of subtle or overt force, domination in (re)production, exploitation and sexuality. According to Omvedit (1990), violence constitutes three basic elements in society motivated by social-historical change; while issues of identity and cultural tradition deal with the articulation in consciousness of the social-material base of society. Violence is conceptualized in terms of what both women and men face in specific forms: oppression, domination, threats, denigration and humiliation. Across space, the effect of violence may come in the short, medium and long term. Hanmer (1978) posits that violence constitutes the use of force and threats as elements binding social processes based on women's subordination. Gender violence issues include both social justice and development, which bring with that obstacles to development of the gender.

However, development scholars have been criticized for ignoring issues of gender violence directed at women. It accounts for a scenario in which women are de-motivated in the development process.

In linking the framework of women's (re)productive activities into the study, a clearer picture of women's exploitation becomes a real issue. Urban market gardening and its associated violence are thus understood using the dimensions of urbanization crisis which Lee-Smith and Trujillo (1992) revealed as aspects of sustainable debate. In this perspective, this work reviews contemporary literature in the Nigerian context.

The historical perspective of urbanization in Nigeria has been documented by several studies (including Mabogunje 1990; Adalemo 1991; Ahonsi 1992, 1995; Aina, Etta and Obi 1994; Onibokun 1990; Abegunde 1987; Fapohunda 1985; Etta 1996). Apart from Etta (1996), which is gender sensitive, a common theme of these studies on the expansion of Nigerian cities barely touched on, the gender violence element, but the areas of potential and actual conflict and violence against women are not clearly documented. However, the patriarchal advantage and state structure. All continue to frustrate women access to factors of production in an attempt to find relevance, for the increasing conflict and violence. so women as (re)producers (Adepoju and Oppong 1994; Horn 1994; Etta 1996), should be provided unlimited access to factors of production if a considerable level of food production is ever envisaged. The experience from this neighbourhood-level study reveals that a dynamic shift is desirable, and that marginality, brutality and structural frustration be tackled by legislation. The process of social justice in the judicial system also contributes to the violence on women. From all fronts the state and patriarchal-induced violence are matters of grave concern which this study challenges. From a city-wide perspective, the growth of the metropolitan area of Lagos alone is linked to the perplexing chains of violence associated with urban market gardening.

Theoretical Foundation

For its theoretical conceptualization, the study draws on three related theories. Spatially, it adopts the location theory which describes the location of activities around the city, as put forward by Von Thunnen. This theory shows that because of a highly competitive land use, competition, conflict and violence are widespread and in the outcome is detrimental to women's effective participation. Because of the humanistic orientation of the conceptualization of the study the method chosen for obtaining data and analysing it empirically, drew on the theoretical approach of symbolic interaction developed by Mead and Blumer (1969).

Second is the human need theory outlined by Doyal (1991), which focuses on social exclusion in arguing that both males and females share fundamental needs to the fulfilment of which are essential to enable individuals to fully participate in the life of the society; these include food production and violence propagation.

Third is Maslow's theory of human motivation (1970) which holds that there is a hierarchy of needs; and among the most basic is the competition for food.

The theoretical base for the study draws further on the land allocation theory, which focuses on the location of activities in urban areas. This is the classic idea put forward by Von Thunnen, applied to the urban informal economy. The issue of land in most Nigerian cities, Lagos included, is a crucial resource for urban farming. The urban expansion, depletes available lands for farming, for example, and this impacts on the scale of violence perpetuated against females, in for instance urban farming. The stress put on land requirement is a veritable source of conflict and violence, men and women are constantly pitched against one and another in a battle of survival of the fittest. However, women lose out because they are structurally violated by multiple disadvantages resulting from patriarchal and cultural sanctions. The urban development discourse is problematic both in theorizing and in empirical analysis which is tangential to the study.

FINDINGS AND DISCUSSIONS

Analytical Context

The focus of this study on gender and violence construction is based on the realm of inequalities in social structure, which is rooted in societal acceptance of male domination, thus propagating imbalances in power relations. It refers to the frontier of women's limited access to resource production and utilization, with discrimination based on stereotypes, beliefs, exploitation and oppression.

The other premise for the analysis is aspects of spatial variations in the forms and causes of processes of gender biases caused by such factors as ethnic and religious persuasion. Gender perspective thus provides analytical premises for understanding the plurality of violence construction.

Land-related Violence

In Nigeria, the concerns of land ownership are the main obstacle to the effective participation of women in food production. Owing to the structural and cultural elements of land ownership, which is male dominated, women are structurally violated in ownership and acquisition. At best, they only farm their (proxy) husband's land holdings. This discourage their total output, because they are continually placed under the subjection of the real (male) owners of the land. This form of structural violence brings with it a form of oppression. This was a common theme that runs through the interview survey. A 42-year-old woman, a former textile trader, mother and currently involved in harvesting and marketing vegetable products from the neighbourhood said among other things:

> ...look around this large expanse of land, you won't see a single woman doing any other thing than harvesting and selling. It is because they say women can't own land. I am very surprised at that because I don't know who made that 'law' and everybody goes about their business as if it is good enough to deny women from having access to land. We work, harvest and hardly have a land we can call our own

'Furthermore, the view below is captured from a 48 year-old woman with her son crying on her back and also harvesting vegetables'

> ... I have come to learn that 'nobody' does anything about the widespread insult and beating some of us are exposed to in this work of farming. The other time here, one woman was beaten by a man for under-pricing a heap of vegetables ... You see... We did not go to school, this is the only farm work we women know how to do very well. We are being gradually chased out of it. Women don't own land, we can't plant or tend 'our own plot of land'. Very soon, we would be stopped from harvesting and even marketing vegetables. This even reminds me, even along the traffic jams in this city, you see young men who hawk vegetable products, which used to be what women do... Those days, men did not farm vegetables, not to talk of selling in the market; these days, men are selling with no shame about it.

The extracts above reveal that women are being structurally and systematically pushed into the operations of harvesting and marketing. At a meso level, migrant farmers say they are violated, they are never allowed to own land and at best are given a lease-holding which is subject to renewal. So migrants are always at the mercy of the customary land-owners. The derived problem of biased access to land and other factors of production by women inhibits their complete involvement in urban farming and food supply.

At the macro level, government policies are unfriendly to urban farming. These include harassment of farmers mostly women, by local government tax officials who also are male. The view expressed by a woman 37-year-old seen tending her vegetable, was:

> ...the other time the officials from the local council destroy my vegetables and use their big lorry to crush them into a rubbish heap... I cried and cried, only to be accused of displaying my products along the road... yet the same government fails to provide us a market where we can sell.

Similarly, a 32-year-old widow, a single mother said that their plight was more pitiable because people denied them what was even due to them. For example:

> ... at first, I thought it was because I used to buy on credit that the men don't sell to me ... So I got a soft loan, and they are still unwilling to sell me their produce... So I asked a very close friend, who later told me that they say I will bring them bad luck, and that it was because my husband died that I even think of selling vegetables.

Socioeconomic Composition of the Sample

In order to obtain a broader perspective of the lived experiences in the neighbourhood, the socioeconomic characteristics are presented here. Of the 40 farm operators in the sample, 25 female and 15 men were interviewed. The average age of the women was 33 years and all had been in the neighbourhood for over three years. The average age of the men was 40 years, with residence over 4 years. All the farm operators were married with an average number of children put at three. Ten of men were Muslim and 20 of the women were Christian, who had no plot of land allocated to them, even where they were interested in farming. All the women claimed they had no plot so they were restricted to harvesting and selling the product from the men's plot. This again puts the men at an advantage to exploit the women with high charges, since the men can always manipulate their supplies. Of the male sample, ten had an educational attainment of secondary and post-secondary level. Within this picture, the male farm operators have farm operators' co-operative union, while the female operators had no union. By implication, the women are not cohesive in their collective bargaining, an instrument widely used in exploiting them.

Attitudes Towards Conflicts and Violence

The interviews showed that the female operators were aggrieved but seemed unable to help themselves. A common theme through the discussion was that equity and justice were most desired. Below is an excerpts from a 30-year-old woman, with secondary education, three children and knowledgeable:

> I have come to realise that 'nobody' does anything about the widespread violence visited on us women here in our legitimate work... most of us women here have little education, and are unable to get government work. This is the only thing we know and are unable to get government work. This is the only thing we know how to do well; yet we are being daily harassed, and everybody goes about their business as if we were not human beings.

From a 43-year-old woman with primary education, a migrant with five children:

> ...we pay to farm the land. After payment, they use all sorts of methods and violence to dispossess us of the lands we paid for... this, I think, is another form of stealing by trick.

From the foregoing, it is apparent that the attitudes of women towards conflict and violence boil down to helplessness. However more they dislike the scenario, no assistance is forthcoming to them.

Below is a comment from the head man of a farm operator, involved in organizing the men.

> ...we think the women should do the selling in the market, so that we men concentrate in producing vegetable... What we give them they MUST buy ... whether they like it or not. That is the way we want and it has been so for a long time. [Emphasis mine.]

Knowledge About Land Management Practices

There exist gender-based tenure differences. Women are major users of farm products as society place on them the responsibility for obtaining food for the family. The dominant tenure enjoyed by the farm operator is that of a leasehold. This gives a derived and temporary right to the land. From a random stratified sample of over 30 farm plots the dominant land management practice was the co-operative farming system, using hired (migrant) labour. This is very effective for the men's co-operative farming. Land access and land use widely affect the individual and collective land holdings. According to the secretary of the men operators co-operative, has obtained a leasehold on the land parcel at agreeable contacts. In all these arrangements, women had little or no say. From a 39-year-old woman, having primary education, with four children.

> Let me even ask you to do a simple count ... you even agree with me that all is not well. Look around here. You won't see any women planting, tilling the soil, weeding and watering vegetables. What they do is to engage in

supplying food to the males working, washing their clothes, harvesting their vegetable and doing the marketing ... this is the situation here.

On conflict and violence resolution, all the interviewees agreed that they reported all cases of abuse to the men's co-operative society which had nominal female composition. In all the cases reported women suffered serious neglect and frustration. An exception was time when a young lady selling rice was raped, and the women came together and arrested the man. He was beaten collectively by the women. Even then, the man was released, though he did not return. The formal instruments of conflict resolution are not also friendly to the women.

Conclusion

The study has shown that gender violence is one factor among many, that accounts for unstable food production. Because of various constraints women face more difficulties than men face in access to the factors of production. There is a real need therefore to develop and emphasise gender-biased land use for food production. Generally, most of the respondents demonstrated evidence of conflict and violence. Consequently, there is a need for change in this area without victimisation. It was also discovered that the men were aware of their advantaged situation in land transactions. When linked with the stress derived from the different land uses, a more enduring conflict resolution method has become necessary.

The socioeconomic factors in the workplace and home and other environmental elements all impact on gender differentially. Therefore, equal access to resources should be encouraged for a more enduring relationship. There should be a relaxation of socio-cultural and legal access to services while appropriate policy thrusts should promote gender harmony.

In the light of the foregoing, the following strategies are suggested:

1. That women's right to land must be addressed and should be based on contemporary realities of open access on gender rights.

2. That there should be periodic reviews of the current situation from the short-run to the long-run, especially factors which promote more co-operation between the genders. In particular, a co-operative process of farm operators should be encouraged.

3. That because of the societal roles placed on women as home-keepers, it is imperative to include women in programs that will improve their lot, especially those that relate to the farming operations of harvesting, storage and marketing. Women's participation will ensure further production of farm products.

4. That community- and neighbourhood-based leaders need to be gender sensitive because the power base is institutionalised.

5. That numerous conflict and violence resolution processes should seek to conform with the contemporary land management practices rather than de-facto management.

6. That support from formal, neighbourhood and informal institutions, e.g., community associations, should address urgently more easier ways for reducing the workload of the women such that they can cope with the challenges of home-building.

Bibliography

Abraham, M., 1995, 'Ethnicity, Gender and Marital Violence: South Asian Women's Organisations in the US', in *Gender and Society*, vol. 9, no. 4.

Abrahams, M. H., 1984, *A Glossary of Literary Terms*, Forth Worth, Holt, Rinehart & Winston.

Achebe, C., 1972, *Girls at War and Other Stories*, London, Heinemann.

Acholonu, C. A., 1988, 'Buchi Emecheta', in Ogunbiyi, ed.

Adalemo, I. A., 1991, 'The Exploding City', text of keynote address delivered at a seminar on the *Movement of Federal Capital Territory to Abuja. The Effects on Lagos*, November, 21-22.

Adepoju, A., 1997, *Family, Population and Development in Africa*, London, Zed Books.

Adepoju A. and Oppong C., 1994, *Gender, Work and Population in Sub-Saharan Africa*, Porstmouth, Heinemann.

Ahonsi, B. A., 1992, 'Population Growth, Urbanisation and Development in Metropolitan Lagos', Background Paper prepared for the *Environmental Problems of Lagos Project*, 1990-1993.

Ahonsi, B. A., 1995, 'Gender, Urbanisation and Environment', Being Literature Review Paper for the *Gender, Urbanisation and Environment Project Phase I*, 1994-1995.

Aina, A. T., 1987, 'The Cities of the "Third World" Today: Changing Conditions, Problems and Prospects for the Urban Youth, unpublished paper.

Aina, A. T., 1991, 'Rethinking the Informal Sector and Urban Livelihood Strategies: The Nigerian Experience', paper presented at the Workshop on *Future Mega-cities: Do Cities Have a Future ?* Saxony, Germany.

Aina, A. T., Etta F.E. and Obi C. I., 1994, 'The Search for Sustainable Urban Development in Metropolitan Lagos', *Third World Planning Review*.

Akande, J. O., 1979, *Law and the Status of Women in Nigeria*, UN, New York.

Alder, C., 1992, 'Controlling and Punishing Women: Experiences of Violence Among Ghanaian Women', *VENA Journal: Women and Violence*, vol. no. 2.

Ashcroft, B., Griffiths, G. and Tiffen, H., 1989, *The Empire Writes Back: Theory and Practice in Post Colonial Literatures*, London, Routledge.

Asian and Pacific Women's Resource Collection Network, 1990, *Asia and Pacific Women's Resource and Action Series Health*, Kuala Lumpur, Asian and Pacific Development Centre.

Atsenuwa, A. V. (ed.), 1995, *Women's Right as Human Rights: The Nigerian Experience*, Lagos, Legal Research and Resource Development Centre.

Awe, B., 1993, 'Gender, Culture, Poverty and Environment', paper presented at the National Seminar on Poverty and the Nigerian Environment, FEDEN and Rockefeller Foundation, National Theatre Lagos, April.

Bacon, L., and Lansdowne, R., 1982, 'Women who Kill Husbands: The Problem of Defence', paper delivered at the 52nd Australia and New Zealand Association for the Advancement of Science Conference, Sydney.

Bart, B. and Moran, E. G., 1993, *Violence Against Women: The Bloody Footprints*, London, Sage.

Battered Women, 1993, An Invisible Issue, in *Women, Rape and Violence in South Africa: Two preliminary studies*, Belleville Community Law Centre, University of Western Cape 1993.

Benokraitis, M. V., 1996, *Marriages and Families. Changes, Choices and Constraints*, New Jersey, Prentice Hall.

Bilson, J. M., 1996, 'The Progressive Verification Method: Toward a Feminist Methodology for Studying Women Cross-culturally', *Women's Studies Int. Forum*, vol. 14, no. 3.

Blackmum, J., 1989, *Intimate Violence: A Study of Injustice*, New York, Columbia University Press.

Blumer, H., 1969, *Symbolic Internationalism: Perspective and Method*, Engelwood Cliffs, Prentice-Hall.

Body-Gendrot, S. L. L., 1995, 'Urban Violence: A Quest for Meaning', *New Community*, 21 (4): 525-36

Borkowski, M., et al., 1983, *Marital Violence: The Community Response*, London.

Bradley, C., 1994, 'Understanding the Problem' (From the United Nations Resource Manual), Strategies for Confronting Domestic Violence; in Strauss, M. and Browne, A., 1987.

Browne, A., 1987, *When Battered Women Kill*, New York.

Bunch, C. and Carrillo, R., 1991, *Gender Violence: A Development and Human Rights Issue*, Center for Women's Global Leadership, New Brunswick, NJ. Rutgers University.

Bunch, C., 1991, 'Women's Rights as Human: Towards a Revision of Human Rights', in Gender Violence, A Development and Human Rights Issue, Center for Women's Global Leadership, New Brunswick Rutgers University.

Byfield, J., 1996, 'Women, Marriage, Divorce and the Emerging Colonial State in Abeokutta (Nigeria) 1892-1904', *Canadian Journal of African Studies*, vol.30, no.1.

Cadwallader M., 1973, 'Marriage as a Wretched Institution', in Landis, J. R. (ed.), *Current Perspectives on Social Problems*, California, Wadsworth Publishing.

Carrillo R., 1991, 'Violence Against Women: An Obstacle to Development', in *Gender Violence, A Development and Human Rights Issue*, Center for Women's Global Leadership, New Brunswick, Rutgers University.

Chinweizu, 1990, *Anatomy of Female Power*, Lagos, Pero Press.

Cleavur, F. and Elson, D., 1995, 'Women and Water Resources: Continued Marginalisation and New Policies', *Gatekeeper Series*, no. 49, London, I.I.E.D.

Connors, J., 1992, *Manual on Violence Against Women in the Family in Commonwealth Countries*, London, Commonwealth Secretariat.

Connors, J., 1994, *Government Measures to Confront Violence Against Women*, in Davies, Miranda (ed.), *Women and Violence: Realities and Responses World-wide*, London, Zed Books.

Copelon, R., 1994, 'Intimate Terror: Understanding Domestic Violence as Torture', in Cook R.J. (ed.) *Human Rights of Women. National and International Perspectives*, Philadelphia, University of Pennsylvania Press.

Counts D., 'Female Suicide and Wife Abuse in Cross-cultural Perspective', *Suicide and Life-Threatening Behaviour*, no.17, pp. 194-204.

Counts, D. A. et al. (eds.), 1992, *Sanctions and Sanctuary: Cultural Perspectives on the Beating of Wives*, Boulder, Westview Press.

Crocker, P. L., 1983, 'An Analysis of University Definitions of Sexual Harassment', *Signs* 8(4): 696-704.

Dabbs, J. M. Jnr., Morris, R., 1990, 'Testosterone, Social Class, and Anti-social Behaviour in a Sample of 4,462 Men', *Psychological Science*, vol. 1.

Daily Nation, 28 February 1997.

Daily Nation, 8 January 1997.

Daily Nation, 9 January 1997.

Daily Nation, 30 June 1997.

Daily Nation, 4 March 1997.

Daly, M., and Wilson, M., 1988, *Homicide*, New York, Aldine De Gruyter.

Davies, M., 1994, 'The Hidden Problem', in *Women and Violence*, Zed Books, London.

Davies, M. (ed.), 1994, *Women and Violence: Realities and Responses World-wide*, London, Zed Books.

Dobash, R., E., and Dobash R. P., 1978, 'Community Response to Violence Against Wives: Chirivari, Abstract Justice and Patriarchy', *Social Problems*, vol. 28, no.5, 1978, pp.53-81.

Dobash, R. E. and Dobash, R., 1980, *Violence Against Wives: A Case Against Patriarchy*, London, Open Books.

Dobash, R., E. and Dobash R. P., 1992, 'Women Violence and Social Changes', New York, Routledge.

Effah, Josephine et al., 1995, *Unequal Rights: Discriminatory Laws and Practices Against Women in Nigeria*, Lagos, Constitutional Rights Project (CRP).

Einsberg, S., and Micklow, P., 1974, 'The Assaulted Wife: 'Catch-22' revisited', unpublished paper, University of Michigan Law School, Michigan.

Eisenstein, H., 1984, *Contemporary Feminist Thought*, London, UNWIN.

Eitzen, S. and Zinn, M. B., 1992, *Social Problems*, London, Allyn & Bacon.

Ekwensi, C., 1976, *Survive The Peace*, London, Heinemann.

Emecheta, B., 1982, *Destination Biafra*, London Alison & Busby.

Emenyeonu, E., 1988, 'Cyprian Ekwensi's *Survive the Peace*, in Ogunbiyi (ed.).

Enekwse, O. O., 1988, 'Chinua Achebe's *Short Stories*, in Ogunbiyi (ed.).

Engels, R., 1972, The Origins of the Family, Private Property and the State, 1884 (edited with an introduction, L. Leacock), New York, International Publishers.

Enloe, C. H., 1987, 'Feminists Thinking About War, Militarism and Peace', in Hess and Feree (eds.).

Equal Opportunities Research Project, 1994, 'Report on Challenging Sexual Harassment: A Conference on Strategies Within Tertiary Education', University of Cape Town.

Erinosho, S. Y. (ed.), 1994, *Perspectives on Women in Science and Technology in Nigeria.*, Sam Bookman.

Etta, F. E., 1996, 'Gender in Urban Natural Resources Management : An Investigation of a Low Income Settlement in Lagos', Research Report, suơnutted to Mazingira Institute, Nairobi, Kenya.

Ezeigbo, T. A., 1990, *Fact and Fiction in the Literature of the Nigerian Civil War*, Lagos, Unity Publishing.

Ezeigbo,T. A., 1996, *Gender Issues in Nigeria: A Feminine Perspective*, Lagos, Vista Books.

FAO, 1990, 'Community Forestry: Rapid Appraisal of Tree and Land Tenure', *Community Forestry*, Note no. 5.

Farley, L., 1978, *Sexual Shakedown: The Sexual Harassment of Women on the Job*, New York, McGraw-Hill.

Fawette, B., Featherstone, B., Hearn, J. and Toft, C., 1996, *Violence and Gender Relations: Theories and Intervention*, London, Sage.

Ferree, M., 1990, 'Beyond Separate Spheres: Feminism and Family Research', in *Journal of Marriage and the Family*, vol. 52.

Firestone, S., 1970, *The Dialectic of Sex: The Case for Feminist Revolution*, New York, Bantam Books.

Folch-Lyon, de le Macorrah, *Focus Group and Survey Research on Family Planning in Mexico*.

Fourth World Conference on Women, Beijing, China, 1995, *Platform for Action and the Beijing Declaration*, United Nations, Department of Public Information, 4-5 September.

Fowler, R. (ed.), 1987, *Modern Critical Terms*, London, Routledge, Kegan Paul.

Frude, Neil, 1991, *Understanding Family Problems: A Psychological Approach*, New Yor'., Wiley.

Gallin, R. S., 1992, 'Wife Abuse in the Context of Development and Change — A Chinese (Taiwanese) Case', in Counts *et al.*, pp. 185-203.

Galtung, J., 1971, 'Peace-thinking' in Lepawsky, R. R., Buehring and Lasswell, H. D. (ed.) *The Search for World Order*, Englewood Cliffs N.J., Prentice Hall.

Gbadegesin, A., 1991, 'Farming in the Urban Environment of a Developing Nation: A Case Study from Ibadan Metropolis in Nigeria', *The Environmentalist*, vol. 11, no.2, pp. 105-11.

Gelles, R. T. and Strauss, M. A., 1979, 'Determinants of Violence in the Family: Towards a Theoretical Integration', in Burr, W. *et al.* (eds.), *Contemporary Theories About the Family*, in B. Hess and M. Ferree (eds.), *Analysing Gender: A Handbook of Social Science Research*, London, Sage.

Gelles, Richard, J., 1987, *The Violent Home*, (updated edition), London, Sage.

Gelles, R. T. and Cornell, C. P, 1990, *Intimate Violence in Families*, California, Sage.

Gelles, R. J., 1994, *Family Violence, Abuse and Neglect*, in Mc Kenry D.C, *et al.* (eus.), *Families and Change -Coping With Stressful Events*, London, Sage.

Gondwe-Kaunda, L., 1990, 'The Displaced Breed: Women in the Traditional African Society', in *Development and Co-operation*, no. 1.

Goode, W., 1971, 'Force and Violence in the Family', in *Journal of Marriage and the Family*, vol. 33.

Hanmer, J and Maynard, M. (eds.), 1987, *Women, Violence and Social Contact*, London, MacMillan Press.

Hanmer, J. and Saunders, S., 1984, *Well-Founded Fear: A Community Study of Violence to Women*, London, Hutchinson.

Harlow, E., 1996, 'Gender, Violence and Social Work Organisation', in Fawcett, B. *et al. Violence and Gender Relations*, London, Sage.

Heise, L. L., Pitanguy, J. and Germain, A., 1994, *Violence Against Women, The Hidden Health Burden*, World Bank Discussion Paper 225, Washington D.C, the World Bank.

Hilberman, E., and Munson, R., 1987, 'Sixty Battered Women', *Victimology*, no.2, pp.40 and 464-5.

Hoff, L., 1990, *Battered Women as Survivors*, London, Routledge.

Hoffman, K. L., Demo, D. H. and Edwards, J. N., 1994, 'Physical Wife Abuse in a Non-Western Society: An Integrated Theoretical Approach', *Journal of Marriage and the Family*, vol. 56, no. 1.

Hotaling, 1980, *Behind Close Doors: Violence in the American Family*, New York, Anchor Books.

Hotler, H., 1972, 'Sex Roles and Social Change', in Saffilios-Rothschild (ed.).

Husseiny, E. I. Z., 1987, 'Violence Against Women': A Case Study from Egypt, National Centre for Criminal and Social Research, Cairo.

Hyden, M., 1994, *Woman Battering as Marital Act. The Construction of a Violent Marriage*, Scandinavian University Press.

Imam, A. et al. (eds.), 1989, *Women and the Family in Nigeria*, Dakar, CODESRIA.

International Labour Organisation, 1972, *Employment, Income and Equality: A Strategy for Increasing Productive Employment in Kenya*, Geneva, ILO.

ISIS International, 1989, `Bibliographic Catalogue on Violence Against Women' in *Latin America and the Caribbean*, Santiago and Chile.

Iyayi., F., 1980, *Heroes*, Essex, Longman.

Jaffe, P., 1986, `Emotional and Physical Health Problems of Battered Women', *Canadian Journal of Psychiatry*, no. 31, p. 625.

Jarvick L. F., Klodin V., Matsuyama S. S., 1973, 'Human Aggression and the Extra Chromosome: Fact or Fantasy'? in *American Psychologist*, vol. 28:674.

Jefferson, A. and Robey, D. (eds.), 1992, *Modern Literary Theory*, London, Batsford B. T.

Jones, 1980, *Women Who Kill*, New York, The Free Press.

Kante, S. and Defoer, T., 1994, 'How Farmers Classify and Manage Their Land Implications for Research and Development Activities', Issue Paper, Dryland Networks Programme, London, I.I.E.D.

Kathleen, L., 1995, 'Developing Rape Programmes and Policies Based on Women's Victimisation Experiences: A University/Community Model in Garber, J. A and Turner, R. S. (eds.), *Gender in Urban Research*, London, Sage Publications Inc.

Kenya Times, 6 May 1997.

Kenya Times, 8 May 1997.

Kimmel, M. S., Messner, M., 1989, 'Introduction', in Kimmel M.S. and Messner M. (eds.) Men's Lives, New York, Macmillan.

Kittay, E. F., 1989, Metaphor, Oxford Clarendon Books.

Knodel, J., 1983, 'The Design and Analysis of Focus Group Studies', in Morgan (1996), *Focus Groups* (Ann. Rev. Inc.).

Kwaak, A., 1992, 'Female Circumcision and Gender Identity: A Questionable Alliance?' *Social Science and Medicine* 35(6):777-787.

La Haye, Tim and La Haye, Beverly, 1995, *The Spirit Filled Family*, Kaduna, Evangel Publications.

Lagos Group for the Study of Human Settlements (LGSHS), 1993, 'The Environmental Problems of Lagos', Research report submitted to the Human Settlement Programme, London, I.I.E.D.

Lambo, E. O., 1994, 'Portrayal of Females in the Nigerian Print Media: Implications for Science and Technology Development', in Erinosho (ed.).

Lauer, R. H., 1989, Social Problems and the Quality of Life, Dubuque, Iowa: W.C.B.

Leacock, E. B. (ed.), 1981, *Myths of Male Dominance: Collected Articles on Women Crosss-Culturally*, New York, Monthly Press Review.

Lee-Smith, D. et al., 1987, 'Urban Food Production and the Cooking Fuel Situation in Urban Kenya National Report', results of a 1985 National Survey, Nairobi.

Lengermann, P. M., and Niebrugge-Brantley, J., 1992, 'Contemporary Feminist Thought', in Ritzer, G., *Contemporary Sociological Theory*, New York, McGraw-Hill.

Leonard, K. E. and Blane, H. T., 1992, 'Alcohol and Marital Aggression in a National Sample of Young Men', *Journal of Interpersonal Violence*, vol.7.

Mabogunje, A. L., 1990, 'Urban Planning and the Post-Colonial State in Africa: A Research Overtime', *African Studies Review*, vol. 33, no.2, pp. 121-203.

Mabogunje, A. L., 1996, *Civil Society and the Environmental Quality of African Human Settlements*, Text of keynote address delivered at the African Regional Workshop on 'The Role of NGOs in the Implementation of the Habitat II Regional and Global Plans of Action', October 14-16.

MacLeod, M. and Saraga, E., 1988, 'Challenging the Orthodoxy: Towards a Feminist Theory and Practice, *Feminist Review 28*, Spring, 16-55.

Mahoney, M., 1991, 'Legal Images of Battered Women: Redefining the Issue of Separation', *Michigan Law Review*, vol. 90, no.1:55.

Mama, A., 1989, 'The Hidden Struggle— Statutory and Voluntary Sector Responses to Violence Against Black Women in the Home', London.

Mama A., 1996, 'Women Studies and Studies of Women in Africa During the 1990s', Working Paper Series 5/96, Dakar, CODESRIA.

Martin, P. Y. and Hummer, R. A., 1989, 'Fraternities and Rape on Campus', *Gender Society*, 3, 457-73.

Maslow, A. H., 1970, *Motivation and Personality*, New York, Harper & Row.

MATCH International Centre, 1990, 'Linking Women's Global Struggles to End Violence', *MATCH*, 11-14.

Mckenry P., Julian T. W. and Gavazz S. M., 1995, 'Toward a Biosocial Model of Domestic Violence', *Journal of Marriage and the Family*, vol. 57.

Mead, G. H., 1934, *Mind, Self and Society: From the Standpoint of a Social Behaviourist*, Chicago, University of Chicago Press.

Meena, Ruth, 1997, *Gender Conflict, A Governance Issue*, SAPEM, April 26-27.

Memon, P. A. and Lee-Smith, D., 1993, 'Urban Agriculture in Kenya', *Canadian Journal for African Studies*, 27,1.

Meyers, M. M., 1997, *News Coverage of Violence Against Women*, Thousand Oaks, Sage.

Mies, M., 1986, *Patriarchy and Accumulation on a World Scale*, London, Zed Books Ltd.

Mojola, Y., 1988, 'Flora Nwapa', in Ogunbiyi (ed.).

Monroe, R., 1970, *Episodic Behavioural Disorders. A Psycho-dynamic and Neurophysiologic Analysis*, Cambridge, Harvard University Press.

Moore, H. L., 1988, *Feminism: Anthology*, New York.

Mosha, A., 1991, 'Urban Farming Practices in Tanzania', *Review of Rural and Urban Planning in Southern and Eastern Africa* (1), pp. 88-92.

Muhammad, Ilyasu, 1989, *Women, the Family and the Wider Society*, in Imam et al. (eds.) op. cit.

National Population Commission (1992), *1991, Population Census: Provisional Results*, Lagos, N.P.C.

Nwapa, F., 1980, *Wives at War and Other Stories*, Enugu, Tana Press.

Ocholla-Ayayo, A. B. C., 1997, 'The African Family Between Tradition and Modernity', in Aderanti Adepoju (ed.) *Family, Population and Development in Africa*, London, Zed Books.

Ofei-Aboagye, R. O., 1994, 'Altering the Strand of the Fabric: A Preliminary Look at Domestic Violence in Ghana', *SIGNS*, vol. 19, no. 4.

Ogunbiyi Y. (ed.), 1988, *Perspectives on Nigerian Literature 1700 to the Present*, vol. II, Oshodi, Guardian Books.

Ojobo, L. J., 1992, 'The Management of the Crisis of Secret Cults in Nigerian Universities', unpublished MPA thesis, University of Nigeria, Nsukka.

Okagbue I., 1996, *Women's Rights are Human Rights*, Lagos, Nigerian Institute of Advanced Legal Studies.

Olson D. H., McCubbin H. I., Barners H. L., Larsen A. S., Muxen M. J. and Wilson M. A., 1983, *Families: What Makes Them Work?* Beverly Hills, Sage.

Omorodion, F. I., 1992, 'The Social Context of Wife Battering in Benin City', in Kisekka M. N. (ed.) *Women's Health Issues in Nigeria*, Benin City, Ramaza Publishing Company.

Onibokun, A. G., 1989, 'Urban Growth and Urban Management in Nigeria', in Stern R. E. and White R. R. (eds.), *Crisis Management of Rapid Urban Growth*, London, Westview Press.

Onibokun, A. G., 1990, 'Urban Research in Anglophone West Africa: Towards an Agenda for the 1990's', in Stren, R., (ed.), *Urban Research in the Developing World*, vol.2, African Centre for Urban Community Studies.

Onibokun, A., Famoriyo, S. and Akanji, B., 1995, Women in Urban Lands Development in Nigeria, in A. Onibokun and A. Faniran (eds.) *Women in Urban Land Development in Africa: Case Studies from Nigeria, Ghana and Tanzania*, Ibadan, CASSAD-Monograph Series 6, p. 9-29.

Oppong, C., 1974, *Marriage Among a Matrilineal Elite; A Family Study of Ghanaian Senior Civil Servants*, Cambridge, Cambridge University Press.

Otokunefor, H. and Nwodo, O. (ed.) 1989, *Nigerian Female Writers: A Critical Perspective*, Lagos, Ostergard, L.

Oxford Dictionary of Current English, 1993, Oxford, Oxford University Press.

Palmer, I. and , W., (1987, *Gender Issues in Food Policy Research: The Case of Java*, Paris, OECD.

Pearse, T. O., 1992, 'Assaulting a Wife: Perspectives on Conjugal Violence', in M.N. Kisekka (ed.) *Women's Health Issues*.

Pinthus, E., 1982, 'Peace-Education', *Quaker Peace and Service*, reprinted from *Friends Quarterly* (Winter), Friend's House, Euston Road, London.

Rakodi, C., 1998, 'Urban Agriculture: Research Questions and Zambian Evidence', *Journal of Modern African Studies*, vol.26, no. 3, p. 495-515.

Ranjana, S., 1991, *Family Violence in India*, New Delhi, Advent Books.

Renvoize, 1978, *Violence in Families*, London, Routledge and Kegan Paul.

Rhodes, D., 1989, *Justice and Gender: Sex Discrimination and the Law*, London, Sage Publications Inc.

Richters, A., 1994, *Women, Culture and Violence: A Development, Health and Human Rights Issue*, Leiden, Women and Autonomy Centre.

Russell, D., 1984, *Sexual Exploitation: Rape, Child Abuse and Workplace Harassment*, London, Sage Publications Inc.

Safilios-Rothschild, C., 1972, *Toward a Sociology of Women*, Toronto, Xerox College Publishing.

Saunders, D. G., 1986, 'When Battered Women Use Violence: Husband Abuse or Self-Defence'? *Violence and Victims*, vol.1, pp.47-60.

Scheaser, S. B., 1981, *Studies in Family Planning*, 12, 409-32.

Scott, W. L. J., (undated), 'Gender: A Useful Category of Historical Analysis', An Unpublished Monograph, pp. 16-26.

Scut, J. A., 1991, 'The Domestic Paradigm; Violence, Nurturance and Stereotyping of the Sexes', *Women's Studies International Forum*, vol. 14, no.3.

Sessar, K., 1990, 'The Forgotten Non-victim', in *International Review of Victimology*, vol. 1.

Shamin, I., 1985, 'Kidnapped, Raped and Killed: Recent Trends in Bangladesh Families in the Face of Urbanisation', New Delhi Conference on Violence Against Women, New Delhi, 2-5 December.

Sheffield, C. J., 1987, 'Sexual Terrorism: The Social Control of Women in Beth B. Hess and Myra Ferree (eds.), *Analysing Gender: A Handbook of Social Sciences*, London, Sage.

Silard, Kathy, 1994, Helping Women to Help Themselves: Counselling Against Domestic Violence in Australia, in Davies, Miranda (ed.) *Women and Violence*, op. cit.

Smit, J. and Nasr J., 1992, 'Urban Agriculture for Sustainable Cities: Using Wastes and Idle Land and Water Bodies as Resources', *Environment and Urbanisation* (4) 2, pp. 141-152.

Smith, M. D., 1994, 'Enhancing the Quality of Survey Data on Violence Against Women: A Feminist Approach', in *Gender and Society*, vol. 8, no.1.

Stark, E., and Flitcraft, A. A. et al., 1979, 'Medicine and Patriarchal Violence: The Social Construction of a Private Event', *International Journal of Health Services*, no.9, p.461.

Steinmetze, S. K., 1988, 'Family Violence, Past, Present and Future', in Sussman M. B. and Steinmetze S. K. (eds.), *Handbook of Marriage and the Family*, New York, Plenum Press.

Stewart, S., 1992, *Working the System: Sensitising the Police to the Plight of Women*, Zimbabwe.

Strauss, M. A.; Gelles, R. J. and Steinmetz, S. K., 1980, *Behind Closed Doors: Violence in the American Family*, New York, Doubleday/Anchor.

The *East African Standard*, April 1997.

The *East African Standard*, 8 February 1997.

The *East African Standard*, 11 February 1997.

The *East African Standard*, 16 February 1997.
The *East African Standard*, 8 January 1997.
The *East African Standard*, 15 January 1997.
The *East African Standard*, 21 June 1997.
Till, F. J., 1980, *Sexual Harassment: A Report on the Sexual Harassment of Students*, Washington DC, National Advisory Council on Women's Educational Programmes.
UNDP, 1995, *Trends in the Status of Women*, Regional Bureau for Africa.
United Nations, 1989, *Violence Against Women in the Family*, New York, United Nations.
United Nations, 1990, *Strategies for Confronting Domestic Violence. A Resource Manual*, New York, United Nations.
Van der Bliek, J. A., 1992, 'Urban Agriculture: Possibilities for Ecological Agriculture', in *Urban Environments as a Strategy for Sustainable Cities*, ETC Foundations, Leusens, Netherlands.
Vickers, J., 1993, *Women and War*, London, Zed Books.
Walker, L., 1979, *The Battered Woman*, New York, Harper Row.
Warshaw, R., 1988, *I Never Called it Rape*, New York, Harper Row.
William, J. H., 1987, *Psychology of Women's Behaviour in a Context*, New York, W.W. Norton.

www.ingramcontent.com/pod-product-compliance
Lightning Source LLC
Chambersburg PA
CBHW021406290426
44108CB00010B/409